ENGAGING
EVERY
LEARNER

The Soul of Educational Leadership

Alan M. Blankstein, Paul D. Houston, Robert W. Cole, Editors

Volume 1: Engaging EVERY Learner

Volume 2: Out-of-the-Box Leadership

Volume 3: Sustaining Professional Learning Communities

Volume 4: Spirituality in Educational Leadership

Volume 5: Sustainable Leadership Capacity

Volume 6: Leaders as Communicators and Diplomats

Volume 7: Data-Enhanced Leadership

Volume 8: The Schools of Our Dreams

THE SOUL OF EDUCATIONAL LEADERSHIP

ENGAGING *EVERY* LEARNER

ALAN M. BLANKSTEIN ✧ ROBERT W. COLE ✧ PAUL D. HOUSTON

EDITORS

A JOINT PUBLICATION

American Association of
School Administrators

NAESP
NATIONAL ASSOCIATION OF ELEMENTARY SCHOOL PRINCIPALS
Serving All Elementary and Middle Level Principals

CORWIN PRESS
A SAGE Publications Company
Thousand Oaks, CA 91320

For information:

Corwin Press
A Sage Publications Company
2455 Teller Road
Thousand Oaks, California 91320
www.corwinpress.com

Sage Publications Ltd.
1 Oliver's Yard
55 City Road
London EC1Y 1SP
United Kingdom

Sage Publications India Pvt. Ltd.
B-42, Panchsheel Enclave
Post Box 4109
New Delhi 110 017 India

Printed in the United States of America

Library of Congress Cataloging-in-Publication Data

Engaging every learner / Alan M. Blankstein,
Robert W. Cole, Paul D. Houston, [editors].
        p. cm. — (Soul of educational leadership; v. 1)
"A Joint Publication With the HOPE Foundation, the American Association of School
Administrators, and the National Association of Elementary School Principals"—T.p.
Includes bibliographical references and index.
ISBN 1-4129-3853-8 or 978-1-4129-3853-2 (cloth)
ISBN 1-4129-3854-6 or 978-1-4129-3854-9 (pbk.)
        1. Academic achievement—United States. 2. Educational leadership—United
States. I. Blankstein, Alan M., 1959- II. Cole, Robert W., 1945- III. Houston, Paul D.
IV. Title. V. Series.
LB1062.6.E64 2007
371.2—dc22   2006019607

This book is printed on acid-free paper.

06   07   08   09   10   10 9 8 7 6 5 4 3 2 1

Acquisitions Editor:	Faye Zucker
Editorial Assistant:	Gem Rabanera
Production Editors:	Astrid Virding and Kristen Gibson
Copy Editor:	Teresa Herlinger
Typesetter:	C&M Digitals (P) Ltd.
Indexer:	Pamela Van Huss
Proofreader:	Dennis Webb
Cover Designer:	Michael Dubowe

CONTENTS

ACKNOWLEDGMENTS

W e wish to express our gratitude to those Corwin staff members who served as our lifeline on this entire project: Faye Zucker and Lizzie Brenkus, our superb editors; Gem Rabanera and Desirée Enayati, their delightful, punctilious editorial assistants; Kristen Gibson, who coordinated the painstaking task of turning a book's worth of manuscripts into a book; and Teresa Herlinger, who caught all the mistakes the rest of us missed. Without their unfailingly patient, knowledgeable work, there would be no *Soul of Educational Leadership* series. All of us are in their debt.

Corwin Press gratefully thanks the following reviewer for his contribution to this book:

Chuck Bonner, Assistant Principal, Great Valley High School, Malvern, PA.

ABOUT THE EDITORS

Alan M. Blankstein is founder and president of the HOPE Foundation, a not-for-profit organization whose honorary chair is Nobel Prize winner Archbishop Desmond Tutu. The HOPE Foundation (Harnessing Optimism and Potential through Education) is dedicated to supporting educational leaders over time in creating school cultures where failure is not an option for any student. HOPE sustains student success.

The HOPE Foundation catalyzed the learning community concept in education first by bringing W. Edwards Deming and his quality concepts to light through *Shaping America's Future* forums in the late 1980s, followed by PBS video conferences on learning organizations with Peter Senge and other leaders. Later, he published the Professional Learning Communities works of DuFour and other educational practitioners.

A former "high-risk" youth, Alan began his career in education as a music teacher and has worked within youth-serving organizations since 1983, including the March of Dimes, Phi Delta Kappa, and the National Educational Service (NES), which he founded in 1987 and directed for 12 years.

He speaks prolifically, has authored scores of journal articles, and has provided keynote presentations and workshops for virtually every major educational organization. He is author of the best-selling book *Failure Is Not an Option*™: *Six Principles That Guide Student Achievement in High-Performing Schools,* which has been awarded "Book of the Year" by the National Staff Development Council, and nominated for three other national and international awards.

Alan is on the Harvard International Principals Center's advisory board, has served as a board member for Federation of Families for Children's Mental Health, is cochair of Indiana

University's Neal Marshall Black Culture Center's Community Network, and is advisor to the Faculty and Staff for Student Excellence mentoring program. Alan is also an advisory board member for the Forum on Race, Equity, and Human Understanding with the Monroe County Schools in Indiana, and has served on the Board of Trustees for the Jewish Child Care Agency (JCCA), in which he was once a youth-in-residence.

Robert W. Cole, proprietor of Edu-Data, is an educational writer, editor, and consultant based in Louisville, KY, and Long Island, NY. His credentials include 14 years at *Phi Delta Kappan* magazine, the last 7 as editor-in-chief; 10 years as president of the Educational Press Association of America and member of the EdPress Board of Directors; 4 years as founding vice president of the Center for Leadership in School Reform; and 11 years as senior consultant to the National Reading Styles Institute. Bob is the editor of the best-selling ASCD book, *Educating Everybody's Children.* He has presented workshops, master classes, and lectures at universities nationwide, including Harvard University, Stanford University, and Indiana University.

Paul D. Houston has served as executive director of the American Association of School Administrators since 1994.

Dr. Houston has established himself as one of the leading spokespersons for American education through his extensive speaking engagements, published articles, and his regular appearances on national radio and television.

Dr. Houston served previously as a teacher and building administrator in North Carolina and New Jersey. He has also served as assistant superintendent in Birmingham, Alabama, and as superintendent of schools in Princeton, New Jersey; Tucson, Arizona; and Riverside, California.

He has also served in an adjunct capacity for the University of North Carolina, Harvard University, Brigham Young University, and Princeton University. Dr. Houston has served as a consultant and speaker throughout the United States and overseas, and he has published more than 100 articles in professional journals.

ABOUT THE
CONTRIBUTORS

Alan Boyle, director of Leannta Education Associates in London, organizes high-quality professional learning in the United Kingdom with world-class educators and collaborates with like-minded organizations in other countries. After teaching in urban schools for 20 years, Alan worked on an English national curriculum project and was a school inspector for 10 years. Alan has always worked in schools with challenging circumstances and has helped to turn around failing schools.

Richard Farson has led several organizations noted for their innovative programs in human affairs. As president of the Western Behavioral Sciences Institute, which he helped found in 1958, he directs the Institute's centerpiece program, The International Leadership Forum, an Internet-based think tank composed entirely of highly influential leaders addressing the critical policy issues of our time.

Long interested in the field of design, he was the founding dean of the School of Design at the California Institute of the Arts, and a 30-year member of the Board of Directors of the International Design Conference in Aspen, Colorado, of which he was president for seven years. In 1999, he was elected as the one public director (non-architect) to the national Board of Directors of the American Institute of Architects.

A University of Chicago PhD in psychology, he has been a naval officer, president of Esalen Institute, a faculty member of the Saybrook Graduate School and Research Center, and a member of the Human Relations Faculty of the Harvard Business School.

His books include *Science and Human Affairs, The Future of the Family, Birthrights,* and more recently, the critically acclaimed bestseller, *Management of the Absurd: Paradoxes in Leadership,* now published in 11 languages. With coauthor Ralph Keyes, his new book, *Whoever Makes the Most Mistakes Wins: The Paradox of Innovation,* was just published by Free Press/Simon & Schuster. An article based on this book won the McKinsey Award for the best Harvard Business Review article published in 2002, the one "most likely to have a major influence on managers worldwide."

Thomas R. Guskey is a professor of educational policy studies and evaluation at the University of Kentucky. He has been a teacher at all levels, served as an administrator in the Chicago public schools, and has worked in the area of professional development for more than 20 years. Guskey has written widely and is a regular presenter at the annual conference of the National Staff Development Council.

Merita Irby is the managing director of the Forum for Youth Investment, which she cofounded in 1998 with Karen Pittman. Committed to increasing the quality and quantity of youth investment and youth involvement in the United States, the Forum supports organizations and communities that invest in young people by promoting a "big picture" approach to planning, research, advocacy, and policy development among the broad range of organizations that help communities invest in children, youth, and families. The Forum for Youth Investment is the core operating division of Impact Strategies, Inc.

Merita began her career as a classroom teacher in Central America and in inner-city schools in the United States. As a senior research associate at Stanford University, she worked on a five-year study of community-based urban youth organizations and coauthored *Urban Sanctuaries: Neighborhood Organizations in the Lives and Futures of Inner-City Youth.* Teaming up with Karen at the Center for Youth Development and Policy Research, Merita directed a multi-site study on school collaboration with youth organizations. In 1995, she joined Karen in starting the President's Crime Prevention Council, chaired by then-Vice President Al Gore. Following that, Karen and Merita joined the International Youth Foundation (IYF), charged with creating its Learning Department, facilitating learning among IYF's Global Partner Network and developing a U.S. strategy, which later gave rise to the Forum. Merita received her Master's in Public Policy from the John F. Kennedy School of Government, Harvard University.

Delores B. Lindsey, assistant professor of educational administration, California State University, San Marcos, is coauthor with Kikanza Nuri Robins, Randall Lindsey, and Raymond Terrell of the video and book *Culturally Proficient Instruction: A Guide for People Who Teach* (2nd ed., 2006). Delores is also coauthor with Richard Martinez and Randall Lindsey of *Culturally Proficient Coaching* (2006). She is a former school site and county office administrator. As a professor, she serves schools, districts, and county offices as an Adaptive Schools associate and a Cognitive Coaching^{SM} trainer and facilitator.

Randall B. Lindsey, professor emeritus, California State University, Los Angeles, is coauthor of three books and a forthcoming video on cultural proficiency. Randy is a former high school teacher, school administrator, and staff developer on issues of school desegregation and equity, and a university professor of educational leadership. He consults and coaches school districts as they develop culturally proficient leaders.

He is a coauthor with Kikanza Nuri Robins and Raymond Terrell of *Cultural Proficiency: A Manual for School Leaders* (2nd ed., 2003). Randy also is coauthor with Stephanie Graham, R. Chris Westphal, and Cynthia Jew of *Culturally Proficient Equity Audits* (due to be published spring, 2007).

Antoinette Mitchell is vice president of Unit Accreditation at the National Council for Accreditation of Teacher Education (NCATE), where she is responsible for overseeing the accreditation process for over 700 educator preparation programs across the country. She is an expert in teacher quality and related education policy and has experience in implementing performance assessment systems in educational settings. Prior to her work at NCATE, Dr. Mitchell was a research associate in the Education Policy Center at the Urban Institute in Washington, DC, where she led evaluations of exemplary schools and school districts, standards-based reforms, and other programs designed to improve the education of public school students. Prior to her work as an evaluator, she taught secondary social studies at Hine Jr. High School in Southeast Washington, DC. She received a BA in political science from Columbia College, Columbia University, and a Master's degree and PhD in education from the University of California, Berkeley.

Pedro A. Noguera is a professor in the Steinhardt School of Education at New York University, executive director of the Metropolitan Center for Urban Education, and codirector of the Institute for the Study of Globalization and Education in Metropolitan Settings. His most recent publications are *Unfinished Business: Closing the Achievement Gap in Our Nation's Schools* (2006) and *Beyond Resistance: Youth Civic Engagement and Social Change* (2006).

Stephen Peters, former classroom teacher, assistant principal, and principal of a Virginia Blue Ribbon School, is currently President/CEO of The Peters Group.

Mr. Peters formerly led the 1,100-student Lafayette-Winona Middle School, once marred by violence and extremely low test scores, into recognition as a Virginia Blue Ribbon School. Through a partnership with teachers and the school community, Mr. Peters and his team conceptualized effective intervention strategies like "The Gentlemen's Club," as a means of capturing children, inspiring their dreams, and giving them hope.

Mr. Peters has shared his practical strategies, philosophies, beliefs, and message of hope with organizations and school districts throughout the United States and has been featured on such television programs as *The Oprah Winfrey Show* and *America America*.

Karen J. Pittman is the senior vice president at the International Youth Foundation (IYF). Before joining IYF, Karen worked for the Clinton Administration as director of the president's Crime Prevention Council. She is the founder of the Center for Youth Development and Policy Research and has worked at the Urban Institute and the Children's Defense Fund. A widely published author, Karen has written three books and dozens of articles on youth issues, and is a regular columnist and requested speaker. Currently, she sits on the boards of the E. M. Kauffman Foundation, Educational Testing Service, and the American Youth Work Center and is a member of the National Research Council's Forum on Adolescence.

INTRODUCTION

ROBERT W. COLE

Teaching children is surely a vocation, a calling—not just a job. Teachers feel called as surely as clerics do, and it's an unfortunate sign of the difficulties of teaching that so many newly ordained aspirants flee the classroom—as many as 20% within the first year, and half within the first five years. If teaching offers rewards, it can also exact a fearsome price. Teaching makes enormous demands of those who would enter its ranks—demands of time and energy, yes, but also demands of dedication and worthiness. Deep demands—demands of the soul.

If teaching is a demanding calling, so too is the work of leading teachers and whole communities of parents and taxpayers in the grand task of education. Principals and superintendents know well the need to be vigilant, visible—to be eternally available. Time is the demon of teachers and their leaders; there will never be enough hours to do all that needs doing. Like any calling, the work of educational leadership has its unique sacrifices. Possibly the most trying sacrifice is that the leader can become removed by degrees from children—the reason most administrators entered the vocation in the first place.

All in all, the nature of the work to be done in schools—lifting young people, readying them for life—necessarily is a work that calls on the hearts, the minds, and the souls of those who work within the schoolhouse doors. In fact, that was originally the organizing title of this entire series: *The Heart, Mind, and Soul of Educational Leadership.* The paring and accommodating that inevitably accompany any joint effort brought us to the title that this multivolume series now bears: *The Soul of Educational Leadership.*

This first volume, *Engaging EVERY Learner,* was selected to send a signal—of all-inclusiveness. Every student matters deeply, to all of us in school and in our society. Subsequent volumes will play different variations by leading thinkers and practitioners in the field on the soul-work of educational leadership. But the overarching theme in this initial volume was sounded by Alan Blankstein—editor of this series, together with myself and Paul Houston—when he wrote, "Saving young people from failure in school is equivalent to saving their lives!" Alan's practical and inspiring opening chapter focuses on "how courageous leaders engage all stakeholders—even the most challenging ones—to ensure school cultures in which failure is not an option for any student. It is not easy or simple work, yet it can be done."

Those powerful words set the tone for all that we hope to do in this series: "It is not easy or simple work, yet it can be done." And more, too: We know how to do what must be done. The work of Alan's HOPE Foundation offers the lessons learned from creating sustainable learning communities, where failure is not an option for any child. This is where our work begins. Alan opens this volume, and then invites Pedro Noguera to take part in a conversation that deepens the discussion. Pedro is a professor in the Steinhardt School of Education at New York University, executive director of the Metropolitan Center for Urban Education, and codirector of the Institute for the Study of Globalization and Education in Metropolitan Settings.

Next, Randall and Delores Lindsey write about "Culturally Proficient Equity Audits: A Tool for Engaging Every Learner." They move from a global perspective of struggles to make the democracy in this country inclusive, to local initiatives for access, equity, and high achievement for everybody's children. Randy, a former high school teacher and school administrator, is professor emeritus at California State University, Los Angeles. Delores, a former school site and county office administrator, is assistant professor of educational administration, California State University, San Marcos.

Antoinette Mitchell is vice president of Unit Accreditation at the National Council for Accreditation of Teacher Education (NCATE), where she is responsible for overseeing the accreditation process for over 700 educator preparation programs across the United States. In "The Emergence of a Knowledge Base for Teaching Diverse Learners in Big-City Schools: From Practice to Theory to Practice," she addresses the school-based solutions that can help teachers succeed with all children.

Stephen Peters contributes "Capture, Inspire, Teach!: Reflections on High Expectations for Every Learner." His passion as a teacher is this: "working with children who at many junctures in their lives had been *eliminated*—eliminated from conversations, dreams, hope, and learning." Stephen is a former classroom teacher at a Virginia Blue Ribbon School, assistant principal at a National Blue Ribbon School, and principal of a Virginia Blue Ribbon School. Currently he serves as President/CEO of The Peters Group.

"The gaps in the achievement of different groups of students have been evident for decades," says Thomas Guskey, author of "All Our Children Learning: New Views on the Work of Benjamin S. Bloom." He asks how we can use what we know to make real progress. A professor of educational policy studies and evaluation at the University of Kentucky, Guskey has been a teacher at all levels and has served as an administrator in the Chicago Public Schools.

Karen Pittman and Merita Irby, in "Engaging Every Learner: Blurring the Lines for Learning to Ensure That All Young People Are Ready for College, Work, and Life," argue that states and communities can change the odds for young people. Doing so, they maintain, requires making fundamental changes in the ways they do business. Karen Pittman is senior vice president at the International Youth Foundation (IYF). Merita Irby is managing director of the Forum for Youth Investment, which she and Pittman cofounded.

Alan Boyle, director of Leannta Education Associates in London, organizes high-quality professional learning in the United Kingdom and collaborates with like-minded organizations in other countries. A product of his 20 years of teaching in urban schools, "Compassionate Intervention: Helping Failing Schools to Turn Around" suggests that we need to invent a way of fixing problems the first time we try. "If the cost of fixing failing schools seems high, the cost of *not* repairing them is even higher," Boyle says.

The final chapter, "The Case for Failure: Risk, Innovation, and Engagement," by Richard Farson, suggests that failure is a necessary step to success. What all of us really need—students, teachers, and administrators alike—is not evaluation but *engagement*. Farson has led several organizations noted for their innovative programs in human affairs. As president of the Western Behavioral Sciences Institute, which he helped found in 1958, he directs the Institute's centerpiece program, the International Leadership Forum, an Internet-based think tank composed entirely of highly influential leaders addressing the critical policy issues of our time.

This volume begins a series that will take four years to complete, and it begins in the proper place: with an attention to the urgent need to engage all young people in the work of learning—work that can shape the course of their lives. Again, as Alan Blankstein says in our opening chapter, "It is not easy or simple work, yet it can be done." It is our aim to help strengthen you for this task.

CHAPTER ONE

TERMS OF ENGAGEMENT

Where Failure Is Not an Option

ALAN M. BLANKSTEIN

The most important thing to know is that the combination of moral purpose and relational trust generates the wherewithal to go the extra mile. It makes a complex, difficult journey doable.

(Fullan, 2003b, p. 62)

FAILURE IS NOT AN OPTION

Most educators would immediately agree that failure is not a viable option for today's students. Although many students *may* fail, and indeed many do, the consequences are generally too dire to allow such an option to be considered acceptable (Springfield, 1995). Students who don't finish high school earn substantially less in wages (Springfield, 1995) and have far greater rates of incarceration and drug abuse than do their peers (Woods, 2000).

Equally troubling is the rise of the for-profit prison industry. In Richmond, Virginia, the local penitentiary can predict accurately the

1

number of prison cells that will be needed based on the number of public school students reading below grade level in the *second* grade (Williams, 2002)!

As an African American woman, Rosa Smith, former superintendent of Columbus, Ohio, Public Schools, felt outraged when she read the statistics on who is being incarcerated; she channeled that feeling into a new understanding of her mission as an educator. It was no longer about teaching math and science, but about *saving lives.*

Smith's ability to articulate such a clear and compelling message is consistent with finding "moral purpose" (Fullan, 2001). Leaders who tap this clear sense of purpose in themselves and others are on the road to developing a Courageous Leadership Imperative (Blankstein, 2004, described in greater detail later in this chapter). For them, failure is not an option for *any* child, and they engage others in building this common philosophy—along with a supportive culture, structures, and pedagogy to make it come alive.

If the success of every child were not enough impetus for education's leaders to develop courageous leadership skills, then perhaps assuring the success of public schooling itself might be. Leaders in Western society have long articulated the close tie between a strong system of public education and democracy (Dewey, 1927; Glickman, 2003; Goodlad, 2001; Putnam, 2000; Putnam, Leonardi, & Nanetti, 1993). Schools are clearly for the common good; they serve as the gateway to, and potential equalizer for, economic and life success for millions of children. Failure is no more an option for the institution of public education than it is for the children within that institution.

Yet our public schools face countless threats. They include the rise of vouchers—even for religious schools (Walsh, 2002)—as well as the concerted entry of large, for-profit corporations into the public education arena. Moreover, it often appears that public policy itself is harmful to public education. Although public officials call for "leaving no child behind," they rarely accompany that call with adequate resources to meet the challenge. Greater courage and commitment are needed now—more than ever before, it seems—to meet these and other grave challenges.

This opening chapter of *Engaging EVERY Learner* focuses on how courageous leaders engage all stakeholders—even the most challenging ones—to ensure school cultures in which failure is not an option for any student. It is not easy or simple work, yet it can be done. This chapter aims to provide many specific steps and strategies that high-performing schools and districts have used to get there.

FOCUS OF THIS CHAPTER

Over the past decade, the HOPE Foundation (Harnessing Optimism and Potential through Education) has been involved in creating sustainable learning communities throughout North America. More recently, HOPE has begun long-term work in England and South Africa, and is currently working with more than 250 schools located in 25 districts within 15 U.S. states and the Hopi Nation.

The work of creating change and short-term gains in a school is relatively easy; the work of creating *sustainable* student achievement is not. Moreover, the work of "educational change is technically simple, yet socially complex" (Fullan, 2001, p. 69).

Much has been written about the technical, structural, and, more recently, cultural side of school change. However, little data are available about (1) creating school and district cultures that engage all students and *sustain* their success; and (2) building the capacity for courageous leadership. These elements are at the heart of our success, however, and they are the focus of this chapter.

SUSTAINING STUDENT SUCCESS

The Challenge in Creating Clarity of Purpose

When it comes to student success, educators face many internal and external distractions in identifying and acting on a core philosophy of "failure is not an option."

First, what is success? In 1949, Ralph Tyler challenged educators to clearly define *what* students should learn as a first step in assuring that they learn it. Increasingly, this answer is being narrowly and externally defined by ministries of education, provincial departments of education, and their equivalents at state and federal levels in the United States. Merely adhering to these standards, however, can create a brain-deadening "drill and kill" school environment that itself becomes part of the problem (Hargreaves, 2003). Even worse, rote learning and other remediation techniques become the steady "low nutrition" diet of students who are tracked into dead-end classes. Once in these classes, it becomes difficult for students to access courses necessary for college (Ray-Taylor, 2005).

By contrast, many high-performing schools are using standards as minimums and are defining success in more holistic ways (American Cities Foundation, 2004). These schools use "enrichment" classes as the norm and provide both high expectations and support for students across the board. They have taken the *external* challenges of student performance demands and turned them into *internal* catalysts for excellence.

Second, which students can learn? No two children are the same: some are poor, some rich; some come to school speaking fairly good English, others speak no English at all. These are real issues, yet they are also distractions from the job at hand. Too often we have heard teachers indicate that they could teach a particular child "if only the parents cared" or "if only the child wanted to learn." Clearly, students come to school unequally prepared, but high-performing schools—even in the toughest situations—somehow find ways to succeed with virtually all students.

Clearly, students come to school unequally prepared, but high-performing schools—even in the toughest situations—somehow find ways to succeed with virtually all students.

Third, who is responsible for all students' success? This question is at the core of determining whether or not schools will succeed with all students. In high-performing schools, we have found that *everyone* is responsible; in low-performing schools, on the other hand, *no one* feels responsible.

In one of the most exhaustive longitudinal studies of school success, Newmann and Wehlage (1995) spent a decade researching 1,200 schools for common characteristics of successful "learning communities." They concluded that successful schools share three characteristics:

1. Teachers pursue a clear, shared purpose for all students' learning.

2. Teachers engage in collaborative activity to achieve that stated purpose.

3. Teachers take *collective* responsibility for student learning.

While these three factors are interrelated (and may all represent a continual challenge for schools), the third seems to be most difficult to attain. The idea that "all means all" when it comes to student success is often held by only a few heroic "super-teachers" in any given school or district. There are also many examples of school- and districtwide successes in creating cultures in which failure is not an option for *any* student. One teacher explained: "How can I give up on them when everyone else already has? We are their last hope."

There are many challenges in engendering collective commitment to all students' success, as the following "case story" demonstrates:

CASE STORY 1

Sidiki

Due to Sidiki's difficulties in school, his mother, Fanta, was called to meet with two of his teachers on Friday afternoon when they had planning time available. Fanta was not able to speak fluent English, and she was anxiety-ridden about the nature of the meeting. She asked a friend who was heavily involved in education to join her. After brief introductions, Sidiki's teachers, who co-taught language arts and history, began to speak:

> Ms. Brown: My concern is that Sidiki isn't very involved in class. He seems distracted, or bored.

> Ms. Lindsey: Yes, I'm not sure he really even cares about what we're discussing. Maybe he doesn't fully understand?

> Ms. Brown: Yes, that's it! He clearly has comprehension problems in my class. I really think he may be learning disabled and needs to be in another setting!

At this point, Fanta, whose English was good enough to understand the gist of this conversation, almost jumped across the table to demonstrate her feelings. She was, instead, calmed by her friend who spoke next:

> "Let me explain the situation," he said to the two teachers. "I have known Sidiki since he came to the United States from Mali, West Africa, five years ago. His father, who is a world-renowned scholar, was recruited by a university to teach several languages native to that region of Africa. Sidiki has

bounced around quite a bit over the years, and is now experiencing abuses at home as well. Nonetheless, he is quite brilliant, and he speaks four languages, English being the last one he has learned." Fanta's friend turned to the language arts teacher to further drive his point home: "Since you are his language arts teacher, it may be that you now speak more than four languages, but remember, Sidiki is only 10 years old!"

The teachers were surprised by this perspective provided by Fanta's friend. They had not seen Sidiki in this light. Perhaps they had only seen the color of his skin, his poor language skills, or his apparent poverty. Although they may not have done anything differently following the meeting, they at least stated their intentions to redouble their efforts and find an approach that might work.

Aligning Teaching Strategies, Structures, Culture, and Philosophy

Although the brief encounter in Case Story 1 lasted only half an hour, it revealed much about the school's culture, structure, level of commitment to differentiated instruction and other engaging pedagogical practice, and its guiding philosophy (or lack thereof). An analysis of these four areas follows:

Teaching Strategies

The fact that the teachers in Case Story 1 were teaming within a double-blocked schedule is among the better practices advocated in education. Yet this is only a structural approach to school improvement; it does not address what happens *within* that structure (see Figure 1.1). In this particular case, the structure was not used to advance best practices in teaching, which call for, among other things, knowing one's students (Ferguson, 2002; Goodwin, 2000) and providing alternative teaching strategies to reach *all* learners (Goodwin, 2000; Haycock, 2001).

The power and importance of the classroom teacher cannot be overstated. In just one academic year in Boston, the top third of teachers (in terms of performance) produced as much as six times the learning growth as the bottom third (Boston Public Schools, 1998). Having strong content knowledge is essential, yet insufficient, especially for teaching minority students (Ferguson, 2002; Grossman & Ancess, 2004). According to Grossman and Ancess

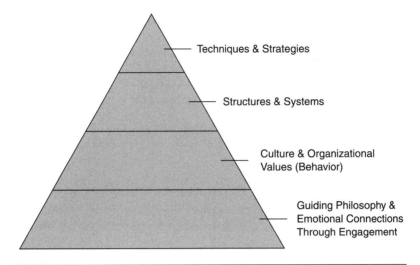

- Techniques & Strategies

- Structures & Systems

Culture & Organizational
Values (Behavior)

Guiding Philosophy &
Emotional Connections
Through Engagement

Figure 1.1   Four Levels of Change

(2004), "The right teacher also needed to reach out to students, encouraging their attendance and helping them see themselves as successful math learners" (p. 71). High standards and encouragement are particularly important for success with African American and Latino students (Ferguson, 2002).

Successful teaching includes the following:

Engaging curriculum. Traditionally, lower expectations of certain student groups (Weinstein & McKown, 1998) have led to remedial curricula that lack intellectual rigor (Gersten, 1996). A study conducted in scores of suburban school districts with high minority populations determined that "scheduling practices can create 'virtual tracks' where enrollment in some classes restricts access to other courses and curriculum." This in turn affects access to selective colleges and universities (Ray-Taylor, 2005). In other words, minority students are often tracked into dead-end classes that affect their future likelihood for acquiring an advanced education.

Minority students are often tracked into dead-end classes that affect their future likelihood for acquiring an advanced education.

Some 30 experts convened by the U.S. Department of Education concluded that top-quality teachers use pedagogy and curriculum that incorporates native language and culture, and they regard students' native cultures and languages as assets, rather than deficits (Housman & Martinez, 2002). Almost 90% of the student population in the Ysleta school district (described below in Case Story 2) is Hispanic; 25% are English language learners (ELL). The district used these characteristics as an opportunity to turn an often-perceived deficit into a strength by creating this mission statement: "All students will leave here with an excellent education, speaking *at least* two languages, and prepared to continue their education at a university of their choosing."

Experiential and service-based curricula can help to remedy the shortcomings of textbooks that exclude or provide unfavorable interpretations of certain ethnic or racial groups. One such project encouraged students to act as ethnographers in order to learn how access to water has affected their poor, rural community. In another project, students acted as oral historians and connected with their own histories by interviewing elderly residents.

Many schools with which the HOPE Foundation has worked encourage middle-school students to tutor elementary students in reading, or support teachers in the instruction of math and science. Attendance of all students involved increased in these schools.

Connecting with students. Good teachers make good connections, personally and intellectually. In order to accomplish this, teachers can pass out index cards on the first day of class and ask students to share information about their interests, their learning styles, and how the teacher can most successfully instruct them. Greeting students at the classroom door, commenting positively on their nonacademic activities, and showing concern when they enter with a "carry-in" problem are all helpful in making connections. Meeting students at the door also helps to identify and prevent potential emotional issues early in the class.

Since so many students are computer literate, questions such as "Can anyone give me an example of something they saw on the Web that's relevant to this topic" is another way to honor their knowledge and make connections.

Calling on students randomly at the beginning of the year ensures their attention. Similarly, drawing names randomly from a hat will eliminate perceived or real favoritism. Eating lunch with students, going to ball games and other extracurricular activities, and writing notes to students' parents *when they are well-behaved* are all excellent ways to build positive relations.

Empowering students. Allowing students to make decisions about classroom rules (and even curriculum) is an excellent way to ensure their engagement. One HOPE school in Texas has created a "micro-society" in which middle-school students choose the "job" they will have during the parts of the day when they are not receiving formal instruction. The instruction they receive supports the "work" they do (e.g., bankers must be able to do math), and they create and enforce through a democratic process their own codes of conduct. There are virtually no behavioral issues in this peer-driven setting, and though the student population is about 80% free and reduced lunch, the state department of education has deemed it a "Recognized" school for student achievement.

Supportive Structures and Systems

Schools often develop policies and structures that are inconsistent with the needs of those they serve. For example, many schools have a suspension policy for truant students. What sense does it make to suspend students who have not been coming to school? Another school in which we have worked dealt with a lateness problem by locking the school doors at 7:35 AM. They solved the lateness situation by creating a truancy problem!

By contrast, highly engaging schools develop their core philosophy and culture around data regarding their students' success, and then build structures to support that success. Another HOPE school, for example, facing a lateness problem, decided to make the first period an experiential education class. Students loved it, learned a lot, and earned their physical education credits in this class. More students came on time, and those who *were* late didn't miss any academics.

Ideally, structures align with the school's philosophy, reflect the culture, and support teaching and

Highly engaging schools develop their core philosophy and culture around data regarding their students' success, and then build structures to support that success.

learning. For example, a pyramid of interventions exists in many high-performing schools to accommodate students who are not succeeding (Blankstein, 2004; Noer, 1993). Such a pyramid is well understood and used by all staff when necessary to provide advance preventions across the board (e.g., to provide all incoming high school students with study and test-taking skills, connections to upperclass students, etc.), and to provide interventions at the high end of the pyramid to students in greatest need (e.g., peer group counseling, intensive assistance in a given academic area, etc.).

Perhaps the most essential structures in high-achieving schools support collaboration focused on teaching and learning (Barth, 2001; Fullan & Hargreaves, 1996; Hipp, 1997; Hord, 1997a, 1997b; Kruse, Louis, & Bryk, 1994; Newman & Wehlage, 1995). As Roland Barth (2001) explains, "I wonder how many children's lives might be saved if we educators disclosed what we know to each other" (p. 60).

Structures that support meaningful collaboration are necessary but insufficient tools for success. They include making time, providing a proper environment, creating advance agendas that focus on teaching and learning, having data to drive decisions, and keeping minutes of meetings.

The most important aspect of good collaboration has more to do with what people discuss and how they do it *within* these structures. Structures are important, of course, but it is the school's culture, based on collective commitments and values, that drives behavior.

School Culture

The culture of a school is demonstrated by people's behaviors. In Case Story 1 above, the school culture was one in which teachers met parents only at the school site and only at times that were convenient for the teachers. Moreover, the teachers had created the clear and simple option of placing struggling students in special education—an option that was apparently used frequently. In short, these behaviors reflected a culture of "do what is most convenient" versus "do whatever it takes."

The culture of a school exemplifies "the way we do things around here." It is based on an overarching philosophy that is eventually articulated in the mission, vision, values, and goals (MVVG) of the school (Blankstein, 2004). For example, Warwick High School in Newport News, Virginia, adopted a philosophy of providing all students with honors classes. This happened over time after researching and piloting "best practices." These eventually made their way into the school's MVVG and became a regular and expected feature of how the school does business: all students now take honors courses.

Following the development of a consensus around the school's mission, vision, and values, high-performing schools often use:

1. SMART goals (Specific and strategic, Measurable, Achievable, Results-oriented, and Time-bound) and clear expectations. Appropriate behaviors, quantifiable indicators of success, and timelines are determined that align with the school's mission and vision.

2. Nonnegotiables

3. Celebrations that are institutionalized to recognize performance that aligns with the school's goals

4. Confrontations when necessary to assure behaviors are consistent with school values and consensus positions

CASE STORY 2

Ysleta Independent School District

The Ysleta Independent School District (YISD), in east El Paso, Texas, has a student population of 46,000 that is almost 90% Hispanic, 25% ELL, and 78% free and reduced lunch. Yet they are cited as having exemplary instructional practices by the Texas Education Agency. Ysleta was the first urban school district in Texas to become a "Recognized" school district for student achievement. However, this was not always the case.

When the current superintendent arrived, he found the sentiment in the district to be that "these kids aren't succeeding because there was too much instability and conflict between the Board and a succession of superintendents." In fact, when Hector Montenegro arrived at Ysleta in January 2003, he was the seventh superintendent in seven years. This earned the YISD the reputation of having one of the worst school boards in the state of Texas. In addition to the various reasons staff had for student failure, there was little understanding of the role the central office played in supporting the campuses. Central office staff were thought to be unfriendly, hostile, punitive, intrusive, distant, ineffective, and isolated. The Division of Finance was nicknamed the "toxic waste dump." There was very little collaboration between schools and site-based decision-making committees (SBDM); that, combined with the turnover of superintendents, created a district of 60 independent schools, rather than a system of interdependent schools.

Instead of focusing on school reform, Montenegro emphasized the creation of a culture of collaboration and teamwork. Staff development for all employees began with how to collaborate effectively. Developing leadership capacity within the organization was critical to making cultural shifts. The staff was encouraged to become more interdependent. Montenegro gave central office staff outcome-related tasks, beginning with enjoyable activities like planning a Halloween party for over 300 fourth graders. He used this as an occasion to further engage his staff in planning activities in the halls and offices, inviting students from elementary schools to come and do trick or treat, thereby closing the "affinity gap" (see Case Story 4).

Lateral accountability was also established, further connecting all within the district. Every month, businesses sponsor a breakfast celebration for the employee and department that provide the best customer service. School campuses vote every month on which central office department and employee give them the best service. The "toxic waste dump" has won in 6 of the past 12 months as of this writing, and is a major contender for winning the annual award!

The central office culture shifted dramatically to one of high-quality customer service to the schools. The office provides direct support to schools during standardized testing (e.g., monitoring classes, providing parking assistance, getting teachers' refreshments); they wear name tags so that all visitors know their names; and they constantly learn together about how to improve services and resources.

This spirit of collaboration and customer service has permeated the entire district. Schools are heavily engaging their own students and staff in creating environments that are conducive to learning. Keeping people engaged, however, is a constant challenge, which is why peers from across the school system work horizontally (e.g., all high school principals) to provide peer review and walk-throughs; feeder-pattern teams meet monthly to align curriculum and share teaching strategies; parents are actively engaged both as learners within areas of their stated interest (such as computer literacy or managing finances) and as teachers within their areas of expertise; and surveys of all stakeholders drive decision making on a regular basis.

Guiding Philosophy

Unlike the Case Study above, the underlying philosophy of the school in Case Story 1 was apparently one that allowed teachers to give up on students relatively quickly. The research and practice on this topic is compelling. Teachers who succeed do not give up on their students; instead, *they* take responsibility for learning outcomes (Lyman & Villani, 2004). As one teacher in a high-performing school culture noted, "It's my fault, not theirs, when they are not successful. I need to be more in tune with what motivates them" (Corbett, Wilson, & Williams, 2002, p. 17).

Teachers who succeed do not give up on their students; instead, they *take responsibility for learning outcomes.*

Likewise, high-performing schools—even in the toughest school settings—embrace at the core of their philosophy the notion that failure is not an option for any child or any subgroup of students (Blankstein, 2004). As Valverde and Scribner (2001) put it, "Unless teachers firmly believe that students of color can learn, they will not" (p. 24).

CASE STORY 3

Developing a "Failure Is Not an Option" Philosophy

In a three-year study documenting schools that embraced a philosophy of "all children can learn and it's *my* job that they do," Corbett et al. (2002) discovered Granite Junior High School. The following case story is adapted from *Effort and Excellence in Urban Classrooms* (Corbett et al., 2002).

Granite Junior High School is located in a poor urban community, yet the students' success rate on standardized tests compares favorably with wealthier schools in the district. This is due, in great part, to the staff's consensus position that every assignment by each student must be completed at a level sufficient to earn a B. In essence, all assignments receive one of the following:

A—Above and beyond

B—The basics. You know your stuff.

I—Incomplete. You need time and support.

To earn an A, students had to complete extra-credit work. To attain a B, students needed to meet the quality standards clearly defined in advance by each teacher. Teachers had to address many structural challenges to make this philosophy work, including how to handle the open-endedness of the incompletes. According to the study, "The ninth-grade teachers established the end of each marking period as the deadline for assignments . . . while the other two grades continued with the more open-ended approach . . . ninth grade also resorted to using C's and D's [still avoiding F's]" (Corbett et al., p. 86).

Granite Junior High School embraced a common philosophy, behaved in accordance with it (culture), and created structures and teaching strategies to accommodate it. In the traditional school's equation of Time + Efforts = Learning, the time spent on students and the teaching efforts (including alternative pedagogies) are shifted only marginally in response to students who don't learn. At Granite Junior High, however, learning became the constant; time and instructional approaches became the variables that could be manipulated in order to assure student success.

Methods of creating a common philosophy vary depending on circumstances, but generally include these components:

1. Development of a core team that is predisposed to the philosophy (though they can and should be discriminating about ways of implementing it). Among other things, this team would learn together and create plans for buy-in by the whole school or district.

2. Exposure/orientation of the larger school community to the research supporting the philosophy. This can be done through studying the data, book studies, or field trips to other high-performing schools with similar demographics.

3. Proving it works at home. Pilot projects are ideal for this. For example, at Warwick High School in Newport News, Virginia (currently ranked 62 on *Newsweek*'s top 1,000 U.S. schools), the idea of opening honors classes to all students initially met with resistance. After a few teachers volunteered to participate, and the successes were celebrated schoolwide, more teachers joined in. Now all incoming freshmen take honors classes.

4. Building consensus around mission, vision, and values based on the preceding steps. It is essential to include all stakeholders in this process, which then becomes an excellent opportunity to engage parents, students, and the larger community (Blankstein, 2004).

When the base of the pyramid (Figure 1.1) is sound and there is consensus around this guiding philosophy, a school can build culture, structure, and teaching strategies in accordance with the collective commitment to, and responsibility for, success for *all* students. On the other hand, if stakeholders vary widely in their beliefs, the best one can hope for in a new initiative is short-term gains and random acts of improvement that lack coherence, commitment, and consistent follow-through.

When learning becomes the constant; time and instructional approaches become the variables that can be manipulated in order to assure student success.

In other words, there must be coherence among the school community's philosophy, culture, structure (including curriculum), and pedagogy in order for such efforts to be sustained. Moreover, sustained success requires an engaged majority of stakeholders moving the agenda forward.

BUILDING COURAGEOUS LEADERSHIP CAPACITY

In the past five years, there has been a growing consensus around the elements necessary to succeed with students who have traditionally done poorly in school. Those elements include the following: engaging curriculum, good teachers, clear goals, safe and orderly environment, high expectations, good parental relations (Carlson, Shagle-Shah, & Ramirez, 1999; Carter, 2002; Holloway, 2004; Johnson & Asera, 1999). Effective leaders tend to focus their efforts, achieve a number of "small wins," and systematically abandon what doesn't work in order to make time for the rest. Courageous leaders create clarity of focus around the core issue of *sustaining success for all students* (Blankstein, 2004).

Peter Block, in *The Answer to How Is Yes* (2002), explains that he is regularly faced with a barrage of "how" questions that serve as excuses for inaction—"How much will it cost?" "How will we get the time?" The hows overwhelm the whys, and inertia takes over.

The courageous leader, by contrast, gets to his or her own "core" (Blankstein, 2004) and helps others in the organization do the same, answering the deeper question, "Why are we doing all of this?" As Heifetz and Linsky (2002) put it, "People are willing to make sacrifices if they see the reason why. . . . People need to know the stakes are worth it" (p. 94).

By organizing people around a shared common purpose, the leader makes the rest of the work a problem-solving endeavor rather than a constant struggle over values and priorities.

THE COURAGEOUS LEADERSHIP IMPERATIVE

As the strategy unfolds, leaders must pay close attention to whether they are generating passion, purpose, and energy . . . on the part of principals and teachers. Failure to gain on this problem is a sure-fire indicator that the strategy will fail sooner [rather] than later. (Fullan, 2003b, pp. 62–63)

At the core of courageous leadership in schools is not only belief in all students' success, but a resounding *commitment* to it (Blankstein, 2004). One of the greatest complaints students share about teachers is the feeling that some teachers are not committed to their success (Grossman & Ancess, 2004; Ogbu, 2003; Zanger, 1993). This is particularly true of low-performing and traditionally disenfranchised student populations (Ferguson, 2002; Ogbu, 2003; Steele, 1999). One teacher shared this story:

> I held out my hand to shake that of every student for months as they came in the front door. Lonnie would never shake my hand, however. One day, after three months of attempts, I withdrew my hand as he entered. He became very upset and said, "Why you do that?!" I replied, "I've been holding out my hand for three months and you never shake it!" He looked at me sadly and said, "Well, I didn't think you'd give up on me like that."

In fact, many students *have* been given up on, again and again, and they expect to be. As a result, they are slow to trust anything to the contrary.

At the core of courageous leadership in schools is not only belief in all students' success, but a resounding commitment to it.

Courageous classroom leaders understand this, and they refuse to give up on their students. Likewise, courageous school leaders help the community to commit collectively and unequivocally to the success of all students. In addition, courageous district leaders foster environments in which "all students' success" goes *beyond* the school.

For example, the Newport News, Virginia, Public Schools, one of the districts in which the HOPE Foundation has been working for the past five years, has turned 18 of their low-performing schools into successful ones by making commitments that go beyond their individual school. Through a paired school model, the entire staff from higher-performing schools actually extend the boundaries of their "collective commitment" to the success of all students, to include the success of two other sister schools. Coaching, classroom observations, collaborative teaming, collective analysis of test scores, and commitments to action all go on across schools.

The Courageous Leadership Imperative (CLI) includes five axioms (adapted from Blankstein, 2004, pp. 19–28):

1. Get to Your Core: Refers to clarifying the driving *internal* core of leadership and the school community. Why are you here and what are your personal nonnegotiables? "Authentic leaders build their practice inward from their core commitments rather than outward from management text" (Evans, 1996).

2. Create Organizational Meaning: Despite the current focus on testing and standards, educators need more than incremental gains on their students' test scores to see the relevance of their work with students. "Reframing" and "cohesion-making" techniques are among several used by effective leaders to help their staff interpret and make meaning of the many initiatives (and the resulting dissonance) often found in schools.

3. Maintain Constancy and Clarity of Purpose: Moves a school toward a disciplined approach to both clarifying and holding fast to organizational purpose. It saves time that would otherwise be spent replacing staff who are dispirited by pursuing yet another "initiative du jour." This axiom also leads to greater success within selected areas of focus, and fosters trust in the leader (Evans, 1996).

4. Confront the Data and Your Fears: "Facing the brutal facts" (Collins, 2001) is often difficult—and can be unflattering! Yet naming and facing fears constructively (e.g., using a data-based approach) can be the first step to overcoming them, thereby expanding the range of possible actions.

5. Sustainable Relationships: Studies of courageous actions in war indicate that it is not so much moral purpose that lies behind putting your life on the line, but the more tangible impact of loyalty to your buddies. "Quality relationships, in other words, are even more powerful than moral purpose" (Fullan, 2003a, p. 35). While school change is not (usually) about putting one's life at risk, the research is clear that relationships are a crucial component of student achievement and school success (Barth, 2001; Bryk & Schneider, 2002).

Engaging the Entire Learning Community

Engagement is the next big challenge in school reform; it is deeper than collaboration. (Fullan, 2004)

Perhaps the toughest part of the Courageous Leadership Imperative is developing sustainable relationships that serve *all* students. For example, we have found that many in the school community have a traditional, zero-sum, win-lose way of thinking: If *your* child gets into Advanced Placement classes, then how does that affect *my* child's chances? If *all* students can take AP classes, then how does that dilute the quality of classes for *my* child?

Moreover, it is very difficult to engage people whom you do not like or whose views you don't understand or don't want to hear (e.g., "You as the leader are part of the problem."). Such challenges often lead to a chasm of communication between parties that lack a shared reality, which in turn leads to even lower affinity.

Many poor practices and inequities often arise because of a lack of understanding on the part of leaders in a school community. To reverse this situation, courageous leaders "move toward the danger"—and then create cultures, structures, and pedagogical practices of engagement as well. As an example, take Carole Day, the iron-fisted African American principal of B. F. Elementary.

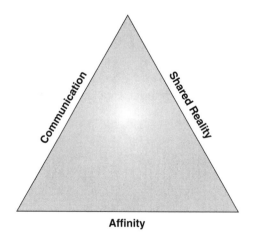

Affinity

Figure 1.2

CASE STORY 4

Creating Affinity

Carole Day was irritated over the incessant lateness of her students, so she set out into their neighborhoods to better understand the problem. To her dismay, she found that many were homeless. She was shocked, and deeply moved, by what she discovered. She developed a deeper understanding of the defiant and disruptive behaviors she saw every day.

Day decided to recreate the culture of her school, beginning with powerful professional development experiences that put staff in touch with students in ways that challenged their stereotypes. She admitted that she herself had no idea of how to work with these students, and she problem solved in partnership with her staff.

Once staff members had gained a common understanding of their students' challenges, and began to systematically engage students in the learning process, students in turn responded; they began making marked improvements in behavior and learning. Similarly, staff were inspired to reach out to community agencies and job-training services to expand their sphere of influence by finding food, homes, and jobs for students and their families. The school went from the lowest ranking of Seattle's 65 elementary schools in academic improvement in 1988–1989 to 7th in reading, 16th in language arts, and 18th in math by 1990–1991 (Quint, 1994).

The principal in this case closed the "affinity gap" by creating opportunities for shared experience, enhanced communication, and ultimately greater affinity. Whenever one of the three legs of the triangle in Figure 1.2 is affected positively, the other two legs will follow. While there are many fears involved with engaging people who seem different in some significant way, the courageous leader finds ways to do just that.

Engaging Students

Unfortunately, too often students and others in the school community are not fully engaged in the heart of the enterprise: teaching and learning.

When students are asked their number-one complaint about school, for example, they generally respond that school is "boring."

Knowing these students and their interests, and why they feel bored, is a critical first step to engaging them. An increasing number of high-performing schools are systematically seeking to understand the needs, challenges, and aspirations of their students. They use student forums, surveys, and focus groups of homogeneous student segments to increase their comfort levels and allow them to speak more honestly and freely in a group of peers—e.g., African American males, bullied students, gang members, high-performing students, and so on.

> *An increasing number of high-performing schools are systematically seeking to understand the needs, challenges, and aspirations of their students.*

Based on these surveys and focus groups, here's what students regularly ask of their teachers:

1. *Be prepared and organized.* Contrary to some beliefs, even low-performing students don't like to lose instructional time (Ferguson, 2002; Haycock, 2001). They like and need organization, as well as a high-demand/high-support environment.

2. *Make teaching relevant.* This is particularly true of students who don't see college as their future. For them, the relevance of the academics and their relationship with their teacher are even more critical than for those students who are confident that they will go on to higher education despite what the teacher does. It is, therefore, these students who need the highest-caliber relationships with and level of instruction from teachers. These are the students who challenge us to the highest level of professionalism.

3. *Show them how to do it.* Students who need us the most often get us the least. Students with greater needs require engaging curriculum, structures of support, and pedagogies that meet those needs. Moreover, assigning homework to students who have not already mastered the knowledge on which the homework is based is unfair. Those students whose parents can crack the "homework mystery" will do fine; those students without such support will not.

4. *Don't give up!* Too often, in the rush to cover material, teachers feel compelled to move on before all students understand it.

This is like the bus driver who, pulling into the station late, exclaimed, "I would have been on time if it weren't for all those damned passengers!" Indeed, students are passengers not to be left behind.

Engaging Teachers and Administrators

Many teachers have difficulty maintaining their enthusiasm due, in part, to seemingly overwhelming workloads, paperwork, and an increasingly regimented emphasis on curriculum and testing. Teachers dislike the widespread, highly prescriptive programs (Datnow & Castellano, 2000), which often diminish their long-term commitment to work (Galton, 2000).

In addition, in low-performing schools, there are often issues of "relational trust" (Bryk & Schneider, 2002) that cause teachers to "go it alone" instead of collaborating with their peers. Likewise, in "good" schools that want to become "great," we find many teachers who work in isolation or have "contrived collegiality" (Fullan & Hargreaves, 1996) instead of true collaboration. Many feel that they are doing just fine; they feel no need to collaborate. Others are competitive; they

Many teachers may seem to be involved, but are not fully engaged with the overall success of the school and each student in it.

don't want to share their best practices with colleagues. Many teachers may seem to be *involved,* but are not fully *engaged* with the overall success of the school and each student in it.

Involved vs. Engaged Administrators

Similarly, principals and district administrators are leaving the education profession in unprecedented numbers due to such job dissatisfiers as paperwork and lack of time for an increasingly complex job. The distance between the ideal and the reality of the job is often great, as evidenced by a survey of principals published by the National Association of Secondary School Principals (NASSP) in 2001. According to the survey, principals feel the most important aspects of their job are establishing a learning climate, dealing with personnel issues like hiring and evaluations, and providing curricular leadership. Yet of the average 62 hours a week they work, only about 23 are spent on these activities. The rest are spent on parent issues, discipline, community relations, and school management (NASSP, 2001; Schiff, 2002).

Principals who are fully engaged spend a good deal of their time outside of their offices—greeting students when they come to school; provided coaching and feedback to teachers; helping teams develop clear direction, protocols, and a culture of data-based decision making; creating a climate of continuous learning and celebration of successes; and confronting behaviors inconsistent with preestablished consensus statements around schoolwide values.

As Karen Mink, principal of O. C. Allen School in Aurora, Illinois, says,

> I make a point of spending at least two hours a day in the classrooms and halls. I begin each day outside, walking among the student lines and greeting students and parents. . . . Behavior issues are minimal because I have a personal relationship with the greatest offenders, and we often have lunch together [when they are having good days].

Similarly, engaged superintendents and district personnel are closely connected to people in their buildings. They provide active support for school personnel, and act as learners alongside their building-level colleagues during staff development opportunities (as opposed to, for example, introducing a keynote speaker and then leaving). Increasingly, district personnel are involved with walk-throughs and classroom observations (Black, 2006). They model the behaviors they wish to see in others, and create climates where learning is celebrated as much as (or more than) sports and other noncurricular activities. In these ways, they become fully engaged with the proper focus of schooling: teaching and learning.

The Need to Reengage

Clearly, if students are bored, they are also disengaged; for them, success in school is an uphill struggle. Likewise, teachers and administrators who feel overwhelmed, burdened with educational mandates, or whipsawed by a string of change initiatives that lacked the buy-in to succeed will also be prone to disengage.

By contrast, schools that have fully engaged their stakeholders create collective energy toward continuous improvement.

(One example of this process is the creation of a common mission, vision, values, and goals.) As one teacher from a high-performing school noted, "When they [administrators] listen to you, you have some ownership of the school, instead of just following orders. So that is going to motivate you and keep you working hard to try new things" (Hipp, 1997).

What Is Engagement?

There is a distinction between involvement and engagement. Many parents, for example, become involved in school activities—often volunteering for bake sales and the like. When schools tap the intrinsic motivations and passions of parents—say, allowing Spanish-speaking parents to teach Spanish after school—they become engaged. *Engaged* parents are energized and energiz*ing*.

Figure 1.3

Similarly, it is far easier for teachers and administrators to gain compliance with rules and regulations rather than true commitment. Think of the classroom teacher who admonishes students to follow rules that *she* has created. What happens when she leaves the room or when a substitute teacher arrives?

Answer: The students are bouncing off the walls!

Finally, consider these quick definitions of the principles that lead to engagement:

Connection: People who feel cared for perform better at all levels (Bryk & Schneider, 2002; Ferguson, 2002). As Principal Karen Mink said of her connection with her teachers, "I may not know all their spouses' names, but I know them all well enough to say, 'You look like you're having a bad day. Are you okay? Do you want me to take over your class for a few minutes so you can have a break?'"

Relevance: As noted above, when the learning or activity is relevant to *my* situation, I will be more engaged.

Empowerment: Some of the most effective instructional reading programs begin with the reader's interests and build from there. Having the ability to choose what one learns, develop the classroom rules, and so forth, is engaging for both students and adults.

Opportunities for success: People need to feel that their chances for success are fairly great, especially when they are trying something new. Increasing the likelihood for success (see Case Story 3) increases the level of participation of all involved.

Quick and accurate feedback: Some students who are supposedly "unmotivated" will spend hours on their skateboards or playing challenging computer games. Much of the allure is the constant feedback, as well as the opportunity for success.

Recognition and celebration: Having multiple means of being acknowledged (most improved attendance, most improved behavior, etc.) is also motivating and more engaging than when the likelihood of recognition is similar to the chances of winning the lottery!

PUTTING IT ALL TOGETHER

The human side of school change can be difficult to grasp, yet this is exactly where the action is. Setting up policies and structures is relatively easy, as is achieving short-term results in student achievement. Gaining *sustainable* student success throughout a school and district is much tougher. It requires building a strong foundation at the base of the pyramid (Figure 1.1). That in turn requires courageous leadership that engages a broad base of stakeholders, including even those whom the leader does not like.

If the enterprise in question were focused on pumping oil or selling soap, it would be hard to muster the deep commitment required to accomplish the task at hand. But there is no more honorable and compelling endeavor than literally shaping the future—touching the lives of children and opening the doors of the world for students to walk through. The ripples that any one of these successful students can create in the world are unknown and unknowable. But the immediate and long-term joy in creating schools where failure is no longer an option for *any* child is the greatest life one can pursue. Hopefully, this series—*The Soul of Educational Leadership*—will help light your path in this enterprise.

REFERENCES

American Cities Foundation. (2004, October). *Best Practices in Urban Education Project: Narrowing the achievement gap for African Americans and Latino Students.* Philadelphia: Author. Available at http://www.amcities.org/downloads/ACFExecSummary.pdf

Barth, R. S. (2001). *Learning by heart.* San Francisco: Jossey-Bass.

Bell, L. I. (2003). Strategies that close the gap. *Educational Leadership, 60*(4), 32–34.

Black, S. (2006, February). Head of the class. *American School Board Journal, 193*(2).

Blankstein, A. (2004). *Failure is not an option: Six principles that guide student achievement in high-performing schools.* Thousand Oaks, CA: Corwin Press.

Block, P. (2002). *The answer to how is yes: Acting on what matters.* San Francisco: Barrett-Koehler.

Boston Public Schools. (1998, March 9). *High school restructuring.* Boston: Author.

Bryk, A. S., & Schneider, B. (2002). *Trust in schools: A core resource for improvement.* New York: Russell Sage Foundation.

Calderón, M. (1999). School reform and alignment of standards. *Including culturally and linguistically diverse students in standards-based reform: A report on McREL's Diversity Roundtable I.* Aurora, CO: Mid-Continent Research for Education and Learning.

Carlson, K. G., Shagle-Shah, S., & Ramirez, M. D. (1999, October). *Leave no child behind: An examination of Chicago's most improved schools and the leadership strategies behind them.* Chicago: Chicago Schools Academic Accountability Council.

Carter, S. C. (2002). *No excuses: Seven principals of low-income schools who set the standards for high achievement.* Washington, DC: Heritage Foundation.

Collins, J. (2001). *Good to great.* New York: HarperCollins.

Corbett, D., Wilson, B., & Williams, B. (2002). *Effort and excellence in urban classrooms: Expecting—and getting—success with all students.* New York: Teachers College Press.

Datnow, A., & Castellano, M. (2000). *An "inside look" at success for all: A qualitative study of implementation and teaching and learning.* Baltimore: Johns Hopkins University, Center for Research on the Education of Students Placed at Risk.

Dewey, J. (1927). *The public and its problems.* New York: Holt.

Evans, R. (1996). *The human side of social change.* San Francisco: Jossey-Bass.

Ferguson, R. F. (2002, December). Addressing racial disparities in high-achieving suburban schools. *NCREL Policy Issues 13.*

Fullan, M. (2001). *Leading in a culture of change.* San Francisco: Jossey-Bass.

Fullan, M. (2003a). *The moral imperative of school leadership.* Thousand Oaks, CA: Corwin Press.

Fullan, M. (2003b). *Change forces with a vengeance.* New York: Routledge/Falmer.

Fullan, M. (2004). *Failure is not an option™ 2: How high-achieving districts succeed with all students* [video series]. Bloomington, IN: HOPE Foundation.

Fullan, M., & Hargreaves, A. (1996). *What's worth fighting for in your school?* New York: Teachers College Press.

Galton, M. (2000). "Dumbing down" on classroom standards: The perils of a technician's approach to pedagogy. *Journal of Educational Change, 1*(2), 199–204.

Gersten, R. (1996). The double demands of teaching English language learners. *Educational Leadership, 53*(5), 18–22.

Glickman, C. (2003). *Holding sacred ground: Essays on leadership, courage, and endurance in our schools.* San Francisco: Jossey-Bass.

Goodlad, S. J. (Ed.). (2001). *The last hope.* San Francisco: Jossey-Bass.

Goodwin, B. (2000, May). *Raising the achievement of low-performing students* (McREL Policy Brief). Aurora, CO: Mid-Continent Research for Education and Learning.

Grossman, F. D., & Ancess, J. (2004, November). Narrowing the gap in affluent schools. *Educational Leadership, 62*(3), 70–73.

Hargreaves, A. (2003). *Teaching in the knowledge society.* New York: Teachers College Press.

Haycock, K. (2001, March). Closing the achievement gap. *Educational Leadership, 58*(6), 6–11.

Heifetz, R., & Linsky, M. (2002). *Leadership on the line: Staying alive through the dangers of leading.* Boston: Harvard Business School Press.

Hipp, K. (1997). *Two steps forward, one step back: The dance of Foxdale.* Austin, TX: Southwest Educational Development Laboratory. Available online at http://www.sedl.org/pubs/cha97/3.html

Holloway, J. H. (2004, February). Closing the minority achievement gap in math. *Educational Leadership, 61,* 84–86.

Hord, S. M. (1997a). *Professional learning communities: Communities of continuous inquiry and improvement.* Austin, TX: Southwest Educational Development Laboratory.

Hord, S. M. (1997b). *Professional learning communities: What are they and why are they important?* Austin, TX: Southwest Educational Development Laboratory.

Housman, N. G., & Martinez, M. R. (2002, Spring). Preventing school dropout and ensuring success for English language learners and Native American students. *CRS Connection,* 2–16.

Johnson, J. F., & Asera, R. (Eds.). (1999). *Hope for urban education.* Austin: University of Texas, Charles A. Dana Center.

Kruse, S., Louis, K. S., & Bryk, A. S. (1994). *Building professional community in schools.* Madison: University of Wisconsin-Madison, Center on Organization and Restructuring of Schools.

Lyman, L. L., & Villani, C. J. (2004). *Best leadership practices for high-poverty schools.* Lanham, MD: Scarecrow.

National Association of Secondary School Principals. (2001, November). *Priorities and barriers in high school leadership: A survey of principals.* Reston, VA: Author.

Newmann, F. M., & Wehlage, G. (1995). *Successful school restructuring.* Madison: University of Wisconsin-Madison, Center on Organization and Restructuring of Schools.

Noer, D. M. (1993). *Healing the wounds.* San Francisco: Jossey-Bass.

Ogbu, J. U. (2003). *Black American students in an affluent suburb: A study of academic disengagement.* Mahwah, NJ: Erlbaum.

Putman, R. D. (2000). *Bowling alone: The collapse and revival of American community.* New York: Simon & Schuster.

Putman, R. D., Leonardi, R., & Nanetti, R. Y. (1993). *Making democracy work: Civic traditions in modern Italy.* Princeton, NJ: Princeton University Press.

Quint, S. (1994). *Schooling homeless children: A working model for America's public schools.* New York: Teachers College Press.

Ray-Taylor, R. (2005, January). Lessons learned about the achievement gap. *School Administrators Journal.* Available online at http://www.aasa.org/publications

Schiff, T. (2002, January). Principals' readiness for reform: A comprehensive approach. *Principal Leadership, 2*(5).

Springfield, S. C. (1995). Attempts to enhance students' learning: A search for valid programs and highly reliable implementation techniques. *School Effectiveness and School Improvement, 6,* 67–96.

Steele, C. (1999). Thin ice: "Stereotype threat" and black college students. *Atlantic Monthly, 284*(2), 44–54.

Tyler, R. W. (1949). *Basic principles of curriculum and instruction.* Chicago: University of Chicago Press.

Valverde, L. A., & Scribner, K. P. (2001). Latino students: Organizing schools for greater achievement. *NASSP Bulletin, 85*(624), 22–31.

Walsh, M. (2002). Supreme Court upholds Cleveland voucher program. *Education Week, 21*(42). Retrieved June 18, 2003, from www.edweek.org/ew/newstory.cfm?slub_42voucher_web.h21

Weinstein, R. S., & McKown, C. (1998). Expectancy effects in context: Listening to the voices of students and teachers. In J. Brophy (Ed.), *Advances in research on teaching, Vol. 7* (pp. 215–242). Greenwich, CT: JAI Press.

Williams, M. P. (2002, September 25). Reading by the second grade is strategy to fight crime. *Richmond Times-Dispatch,* p. H4.

Zanger, V. (1993). Academic costs of Latino students' perceptions at a Boston high school. In R. Rivera & S. Nieto (Eds.), *The education of Latino students in Massachusetts: Issues, research, and policy implications* (pp. 170–190). Amherst: University of Massachusetts Press.

CHAPTER TWO

FROM VISION
TO REALITY

Pedro Noguera Discusses Engaging
Every Learner With Alan Blankstein

PEDRO A. NOGUERA AND
ALAN M. BLANKSTEIN

On June 15, 2006, Alan Blankstein invited Pedro Noguera to discuss the role of educational leaders in engaging every learner.

Question from Alan Blankstein: What are some specific strategies that districts or schools can use to ensure that parents hold schools accountable? Why is it important for families to hold schools accountable? How do you "teach accountability"?

Professor Noguera: In most suburban and affluent communities, schools are first and foremost accountable to the parents they serve. No law says that this must be the case, but middle-class parents have a keen sense of their rights as taxpayers and voters, and their sense of entitlement leads them to believe that they can make demands of the schools that serve their children.

In most urban and low-income communities, this is not the case. Schools are accountable only to district administrators or state officials, people they typically do not interact with on a regular basis. The schools may serve poor children, but they generally do not feel particularly accountable to their parents. In some cases, there may even be antagonistic relations between parents and schools due to distrust and a lack of belief that the schools are taking care of the interests of the children.

Whenever schools believe that parents are irrelevant, or that there is no need to be responsive to their needs or expectations, children usually suffer. This is because parents are generally the best advocates of and for their children.

Q: How should education leaders engage family and community support on specific reform efforts? What are the specific steps these leaders take? How will the leaders know that they are successful in getting that support?

Professor Noguera: Educational leaders who are serious about enlisting parents as partners in the educational process—and all of the research says that such a partnership is essential if we are to raise student achievement—must start by asking, what do we expect of the parents we serve and what can they expect from us?

Children benefit most when there is a sense of what James Coleman described as social closure, or mutual responsibility and reinforcement of educational priorities between parents and schools. Such a partnership must be based upon the recognition that all parents, regardless of their income or level of education, can help their children, and the vast majority of parents would like to see their children succeed.

It helps if the first point of contact with parents is not a message home about a problem, but rather an attempt to become acquainted.

The first step is for educational leaders to convey to parents that they truly want the best for their children and are willing to be held accountable. In turn, they must be explicit in asking parents to play an active role in supporting their children. It helps if the first point of contact with parents is not a message home about a problem, but rather an attempt to become acquainted. Schools should also devise a variety of activities throughout the school year to involve parents. Student presentations, translation services, childcare, and food and transportation may all be necessary if parents are to be involved.

Q: How does a leader share a vision with the community? How would that leader know that the vision is truly shared?

Professor Noguera: The leader should share his or her vision by meeting regularly with community members in a variety of settings: churches, house meetings, civic groups, and so forth. The vision must address the real concerns and challenges parents in that community face, and it must be combined with a plan for how the vision will be realized. The plan should be simple and clear enough that it can be handed out on a single page and explained relatively quickly. The plan should also include an explicit role for parents and, of course, there should be ample opportunity for parents to respond, question, and be included in planning efforts.

Q: You once spoke of a perception that there is a zero-sum game in the allocation of resources. More resources for some mean less for others. How do effective leaders change that perception?

Professor Noguera: In many schools, there is a perception that if we do more for the struggling students, it will come at the expense of services for more successful students. This is often an issue in suburban communities that are trying to address the achievement gap, and that recognize that tracking and other forms of ability grouping may have been historically to deny poor children, and children of color generally, access to rigorous programs.

The goal should be to expand access to rigorous courses, increase support for students who need it (so that they are not set up for failure), and make sure that no children have been relegated to an inferior education because they have been assigned the worst teachers.

The goal should be to expand access to rigorous courses, increase support for students who need it (so that they are not set up for failure), and make sure that no children have been relegated to an inferior education because they have been assigned the worst teachers. It is a vision that combines a commitment to academic excellence with one rooted in unflinching support for equity.

Q: You often cite research that says that schools can change their structure and organization, but unless they reform their cultures, nothing will change in student achievement. What is the difference between changing structure and changing cultures?

Professor Noguera: School culture is about values, norms, attitudes, beliefs, and relationships. Most reforms ignore these and focus instead on organization, structure, and curriculum. While these are important, unless there is a change in culture, typically nothing changes.

Q: How should the leader go about changing culture?

Professor Noguera: Leaders can attempt to transform school culture by engaging all members of the school community—teachers, parents, and students—in thoughtful discussions about the goals of education and about what each party must do to achieve these. Schoolwide retreats may help in allowing for such discussions. There must also be a willingness to adopt routines that reinforce key school values. Ceremonies that recognize significant achievements, the recitation of an inspiring poem or slogan, a school motto, or a particular approach to staff meetings all can serve as ways to reinforce the values, ideals, and principles that the school holds dear. Ultimately, changing school culture requires "buy-in" from all of the core constituencies and consistency in acting upon the vision and goals.

Q: What kinds of cultures commonly exist in schools?

Professor Noguera: In many schools, there is a culture of complacency about school outcomes. When there are predictable patterns of achievement (e.g., most minority students not doing well, or many immigrant students dropping out), this failure can be "normalized" and accepted as natural. Some schools may also have highly dysfunctional cultures where there is abuse of children or teachers, where adults are unwilling to accept responsibility for student outcomes, and where parents are distrustful of educators.

Q: Should the leaders' approach to changing each of these kinds of cultures be different? What specifically should a leader do to shift school culture? How will the leader know if he or she has the kind of school culture that is effective? What indicators should the leader look for? What should he or she monitor on a regular basis and how? What systems should be put in place? Can you give examples of high-performing cultures and other, more common cultures?

Professor Noguera: The first step in changing a culture is getting buy-in from the staff about the goals, the vision, and the steps that will be taken to get there. This requires time for thoughtful deliberation. Once a plan is agreed upon, there must be a specific plan for implementation that lays out what each party must do. It is very important for the leader to recognize that every party in the school, including the students, must be engaged in adopting new approaches to schooling.

The plan should include measurable benchmarks that can be used to evaluate whether or not the goals are being achieved. This could include better attendance, fewer disciplinary referrals or

It is very important for the leader to recognize that every party in the school, including the students, must be engaged in adopting new approaches to schooling.

tardies, and so forth. Cultures are rooted in rituals, and the activities that will be used to ground the culture should be agreed upon and treated as sacred. For example, at one elementary school in Virginia Beach, the principal and a teacher greet each student at the door every morning as he or she enters the building. At a high school in Manhattan, a staff meeting is held each morning to "check in" about how things are going and to discuss upcoming events.

Q: What should the leader do about resistant or disenchanted teachers who use the failings of previous school reform efforts to avoid engaging in the "newest" reform effort? What are some reasons for and strategies to address resistance?

Professor Noguera: Some resistance is healthy. Teachers know that many reforms are not well thought out and are never evaluated. They also know that if they close their classroom door, they can usually outlast any reform.

However, some resistance is designed to undermine positive change. In this case, principals must figure out which teachers support their goals (and encourage these allies to take an active role in the change process), which teachers are neutral, and which ones are adamantly opposed. The goal is to win over those in the middle and isolate the opposition. In some cases, it may be necessary to have some staff moved if they prove to be too much of an obstacle to change.

Q: There are a number of reform efforts out there that claim success. What are the common characteristics of successful school reform efforts?

Professor Noguera: Reforms that are successful achieve buy-in from the people who will have to carry them out, namely teachers and kids. Without this, it doesn't matter how good the idea may be. Reforms that provide coherence and consistency in the school's approach to instruction, assessment, discipline, advising, and other key elements generally have a positive impact on learning outcomes.

---------- ✂ ----------

Reforms that are successful achieve buy-in from the people who will have to carry them out, namely teachers and kids. Without this, it doesn't matter how good the idea may be.

Q: Since no teaching or learning takes place in the central office, what should educational leaders be doing to make sure they are helping schools and students and not making their lives more difficult?

Professor Noguera: Instructional leaders must be present in the classroom on a regular basis and not just when evaluations are scheduled. Principals must also provide teachers with opportunities to learn from each other through observation, time to meet to share plans and ideas, and opportunities to understand whole-school data.

Q: What would happen to an effective school if the central office disappeared? How can a school do well if the central office isn't helping or is going in a nonproductive direction?

Professor Noguera: Many districts are considering changing the role of the central office by developing a more radical form of site-based management wherein schools can purchase services from the central office or go elsewhere. This is based upon a successful model from Winnipeg that is now being touted by the Broad Foundation. New York and Oakland are in the midst of such reforms.

In districts where the central office still has a role, it should primarily be one of providing the assistance that schools need to be successful. Anything that is not helpful or that detracts from the school's mission should be ceased, and this includes most meetings held at the central office.

---------- ✂ ----------

Anything that is not helpful or that detracts from the school's mission should be ceased, and this includes most meetings held at the central office.

Q: What will the "future" superintendent be doing that a current superintendent is not doing? What challenges will future superintendents have to overcome in the next 10 years?

Professor Noguera: In many districts, the primary job of the superintendent is public relations and managing the school board.

While this role is important, in the future superintendents will have to have a more hands-on approach and will have to do more adaptive work, particularly in responding to the needs of troubled schools. They also should be involved in audits to ensure that financial priorities are aligned with educational needs, and they should actively engage the community in providing tangible support for the school.

Q: What are some examples of "adaptive work"?

Professor Noguera: The adaptive work is focused on responding to changes that are occurring in the external environment. For example, if you are in a district that has recently experienced a significant increase in immigrant students, the adaptive work forces us to get to know the community and its leaders, to identify agencies that can help with outreach and translation, and to find ways to establish relations with parents. Adaptive work is never routinized. It is always based on understanding that the challenges we face in educating children require ongoing reflection on the goals and strategies utilized to meet student needs.

Adaptive work is never routinized. It is always based on understanding that the challenges we face in educating children require ongoing reflection on the goals and strategies utilized to meet student needs.

Q: How does an education leader fill the gap between vision and reality?

Professor Noguera: With planning. Good, thorough planning combined with a willingness to evaluate the implementation of plans is essential.

Acknowledgment: The authors and publisher thank Michael Simms for his contributions to this chapter.

CHAPTER THREE

CULTURALLY PROFICIENT EQUITY AUDITS

A Tool for Engaging Every Learner

DELORES B. LINDSEY AND RANDALL B. LINDSEY

> ... *a high-quality public school system is essential, not only for parents who send their children to these schools but also for the public good as a whole.*
>
> (Fullan, 2003, p. 4)

In this chapter, we hope to guide readers from a global perspective of struggles to make the democracy in this country inclusive, to local initiatives for access, equity, and high achievement for everybody's children. We wish to foster discussions and actions that lead to more students than ever before achieving at higher levels than ever before. Our students at every grade level—from preschool through high school—depend on the adult communities of teachers, counselors, administrators, and parents/guardians to create environments and conditions in which each student experiences academic success. The current achievement gap data (Perie, Moran, Lutkus, & Tirre, 2005) reflect the need for inclusive discussions that enable educators to play a key role in the intentional unfolding of a democracy in such a way that students who graduate from our P–12 schools

- are able to function at high academic levels,
- are able to function well in our increasingly diverse society, and
- have a palpable sense of their own cultures.

Since 2001, school districts throughout the United States have been mandated to follow the doctrine of the No Child Left Behind Act (NCLB). Though several states had implemented similar programs prior to 2001, NCLB has drawn concerted national attention to the disparities of achievement among demographic groups. Throughout the country, many school districts receiving federal funds for educating students of poverty (e.g., Title I) have used this mandate as an opportunity to examine student achievement data in ways that clearly identify the achievement gaps that exist between students who have been historically well served by our schools and those who have been marginalized in many ways. Recent

Are educators trying to close the testing *gap or the* achievement *gap?*

data from the National Association of Educational Progress indicate that districts all across the country are using assessment data to inform decisions about curriculum, instruction, and learning outcomes and are making headway in narrowing the gap (Perie et al., 2005; "Quality Counts at 10," 2006). Other districts struggle in closing the gap because educators often blame students for their family and social circumstances. These educators hold beliefs based on negative racial, social, and cultural stereotypes about who learns and at what levels students can achieve.

A conundrum exists for many school leaders as they are faced with this question: Are educators trying to close the *testing* gap or the *achievement* gap? Early in the standards reform movement, the development of standards-based systems was seen as a way to ensure that each student could achieve progress toward a common set of learner goals as measured by standardized achievement tests.

Recently, however, the conversation has developed among researchers and educators as to whether school improvement is grounded in educational standards or standardized assessments (Haycock, Jerald, & Huang, 2001; Stiggins, 2005). The controversy deepens as school districts use federal- and state-funded programs required to deliver a *scientific, research-based curriculum* designed to improve reading and math achievement for all students. Curriculum is often developed and content delivered according to strict, state-mandated, state-adopted curriculum, textbooks, and assessment tools, with little opportunity given for teachers to differentiate and enhance the instructional approaches and materials of instruction to maximize the success of all students ("Quality Counts at 10," 2006).

All too often, individual students or groups of students who are identified as *needing improvement* are removed from their elective courses, visual and performing arts courses, or applied arts and sciences and are assigned double doses of reading and mathematics. These students are often selected for intensive coursework in reading and mathematics because, based on standardized test results, they are close to the cutoff scores. The students may show enough improvement to move up into the next range of scores and make the school appear to be successful—but have they been denied access and meaningful learning opportunities in other subjects? What assessment tools and additional means of measuring student achievement are available for educators to use so that diverse learning styles, cultural background, and multiple perspectives are valued and reflected in the assessment strategies and instruments? These questions and accompanying risks face us as we make decisions about who has the opportunity to learn.

CLOSING THE GAP: COMPELLED BY LAW OR MORAL IMPERATIVE?

Long before the enactment of NCLB in 2001, the student achievement gap existed between predominantly white, affluent students and students of poverty and color. One of the disquieting aspects of both state and federal reform initiatives is that the reforms have been legislatively imposed on our profession. The fact that, historically, educators have not been required by law to disaggregate and examine testing data according to the demographic makeup of the school did not absolve us of the responsibility for educating *all* students without respect to their race, ethnicity, social class, gender, or sexual orientation. Now that we are faced with verifiable data that clearly identify students who are not being well served, as educators we can no longer ignore the needs of these learners. Our moral integrity is at risk when, as the very resource that parents trust will care for their children and prepare them for a productive future, we wait to see what the next mandate will be from the statehouse rather than teach in ways that are culturally responsive.

A Brief History of Equality and Equity

When the formal government for the United States was created in 1789, the people who had the right to vote were property-owning white males. Large segments of the population were denied this most basic of democratic rights—African slaves, People of the First Nation, freedmen, women, and non–property-owning white men. By the middle of the 19th century, the right to vote had been extended to white males universally.

The corollary to the perquisite of the right to vote was having access to an education. In the first half of the 19th century, formal education was almost universally limited to those who could afford to attend private or parochial schools. An egregious example of how education was denied to large segments of the population was the prohibition in many slave states that made it illegal for African slaves to learn to read (Douglass, 1960). One bright spot for access to education occurred in Massachusetts. Horace Mann, as the First Secretary for the Board of Education, argued for a free public education for every child and led that state to enact the first U.S. compulsory education law in 1852.

European immigrants from the mid-19th to the early 20th century included droves of people from Ireland, Germany, Italy, and Eastern Europe. These immigrant groups each entered U.S. society near the bottom rung of the social-class ladder and in two to three generations were themselves well-represented in the burgeoning

Exploited as many immigrants were, they entered the United States with rights and privileges not afforded to People of the First Nation or to African Americans.

middle class. It is sad to note that, exploited as many of these immigrants were, they entered the United States with rights and privileges not afforded to People of the First Nation or to African Americans (Takaki, 1993).

At the beginning of the 20th century, few of what we now call school-age populations were attending school beyond the sixth grade. The industrialization of the first half of the 20th century and the technological explosion that followed World War II set the stage for the comprehensive school system that we have today. In fact, mandatory universal education through Grade 12 is a very modern occurrence. As of 2002, a total of 27 states have compulsory education requirements only to the attainment of age 16 (Snyder, 2005). This spiraling effect of who was educated in our schools—public, private, independent, or parochial—has laid the foundation for many of the inequities that are now evident.

Since the 1960s, Mexican Americans, African Americans, Asian Americans, and women have had to resort to legal processes to gain access to the same education afforded middle-class, white males. These legislative processes and court decisions—among them, *Mendez* v. *Westminster* (1947), *Brown* v. *Topeka Board of Education* (1954, 1955), the 1964 Civil Rights Act, *Lau* v. *Nichols* (1974), and Title IX of the Education Amendments of 1972—are representative of the extent to which nondominant groups have had to struggle for access to equitable educational opportunities.

Our complicity in the neglect of the educational needs of identified groups of citizens has not been due to lack of information.

The corollary to this resistance is that we in the education community initiated none of the legislative or judicial reviews to remedy these inequities in access to education. In reality, we have been guilty of complicitly resisting the access of nondominant groups to educational opportunities and experiences.

Our complicity in the neglect of the educational needs of identified groups of citizens has not been due to lack of information. From the popular press to government-commissioned studies to current, prominent journal articles, descriptions about the barriers to access have been abundantly available. Ralph Ellison's seminal work, *Invisible Man* (1951), viewed our society through the lens of an African American male; it should have awakened us. However, although Ellison's novel was read widely in the 1950s, and still appears on many high school and college American literature reading lists, its message of *invisibility* appears to not have resonated with people in the dominant group. Tom Carter's (1970) studies conducted for the U.S. Civil Rights Commission documented the educational neglect directed toward Mexican Americans. And, in a recent issue of *Phi Delta Kappan,* Starnes (2006) traces the history of neglect experienced by First Nation People and the importance of educators knowing the history and culture of students who are different from themselves.

In brief, this brings us to the dawn of the 21st century and the various state and federal initiatives designed to bridge the achievement gaps. Most state initiatives focus on all public schools while the federal initiative under the Elementary and Secondary Education Act reauthorization, widely known as No Child Left Behind (2001), is confined to schools receiving Title I funds. If NCLB and the state initiatives have any redeeming social value, it is that they call attention to the *elephant in the middle of the room* that institutional policy makers and educators have pretended not to see for the past 50 years: namely, that children and youth from low-income, African American, Latino, People of the First Nation, and English-learning families lag behind assimilated, middle-class students in reading and mathematics achievement.

The Full Extent of the Achievement Gaps

We have two significant achievement gaps in the United States. The most prominently discussed academic achievement gap is that of nondominant groups of students—the poor, those struggling to learn to speak English, African Americans, Latinos, and First Nation People. In reality, our schools work relatively well for the students for whom they were designed but are struggling to serve all other students ("Quality Counts at 10," 2006; Wartell & Huelskamp, 1991). That the disparities are rooted in racist, ethnocentric, and sexist context of the past and present is rarely discussed in policy-making or educational circles.

It is important to note that there is a second achievement gap that most educational policy makers and educators either cannot see or choose not to see. The second, often unacknowledged achievement gap is a result of the dominant group's inability to see the roadblocks that have been, and are, placed in the way of members of nondominant socioeconomic, racial, ethnic, gender, or language groups. This selective invisibility leads to a sense of privilege and entitlement for members of the dominant group. Whereas systems of oppression impose barriers for members of nondominant groups, concomitant systems of privilege and entitlement impose barriers for members of the dominant group.

The barriers erected by a sense of privilege and entitlement involve a skewed sense of reality.

The barriers erected by a sense of privilege and entitlement involve a skewed sense of reality that can retard one's ability to pursue ethical and moral avenues in meeting the academic and social needs of nondominant groups.

The position of privilege often allows educators to voice biased or ill-informed assumptions about parents from nondominant groups. Typical of such assumptions are comments such as the following:

> "Their parents won't come to parent conferences because they don't care about the education of their children."

> "Why try to help them? They will end up being gang bangers, just like their fathers!"

> "Why should I learn anything about their culture? This is America—let them learn about us!"

Educators who make comments like the ones above are in need of different lenses, tools, and structures that support and invite ways to surface these assumptions and values and begin to change them. Educators must engage in intentional conversations about how parents and students who are different from themselves behave and learn. One approach is *cultural proficiency,* a lens for inclusion of all learners.

THE LENS OF CULTURAL PROFICIENCY

Cultural proficiency (Cross, Bazron, Dennis, & Isaacs, 1989; Lindsey, Nuri Robins, & Terrell, 2003; Nuri Robins, Lindsey,

Lindsey, & Terrell, 2006) provides a nonthreatening, comprehensive, systemic structure within which school leaders can discuss issues facing their schools. The four tools of cultural proficiency provide the means to assess and change one's own values and behaviors and an organization's policies and practices in a way that serves our society and allows the continuing unfolding of our democracy. From 1789 to today, the struggle to serve the needs of a diverse society has continued. Our school systems can and should have a prominent leadership role in creating a moral and ethical democracy.

The Tools of Cultural Proficiency

Effective use of the matrices presented in this chapter is predicated on one's knowing and understanding the four tools of cultural proficiency (Cross et al., 1989; Lindsey et al., 2003; Nuri Robins et al., 2006). The tools of cultural proficiency—the guiding principles, the barriers, the continuum, and the essential elements—combine to provide a framework for analyzing your own values and behaviors, as well as your school's policies and practices.

> *Our school systems can and should have a prominent leadership role in creating a moral and ethical democracy.*

In this section, we summarize salient features of each of the tools and how they support the relevance and utility of the matrices. The guiding principles and the barriers provide a context for development of the matrices. The continuum and the essential elements provide the specific tools for constructing the matrices.

The Guiding Principles of Cultural Proficiency

The guiding principles provide a framework for the examination of the core values of schools and how espoused theory and theory in action differ when schools are undergoing academic audits (Argyris, 1990; Schein, 1989). The guiding principles are the following:

- Culture is a predominant force in the lives of people and organizations.
- People are served in varying degrees by the dominant culture.
- People have both group identities and individual identities.

- Diversity within cultures is vast and significant.
- Each cultural group has unique cultural needs.

In Nuri Robins et al. (2006), the authors noted that

understanding and acknowledging the five principles and choosing to manifest them in your behavior are demonstrations of culturally proficient leadership. The choice you make to align your leadership actions with the five principles of cultural proficiency communicates a strong message throughout your school's community that you value diversity and fully expect that every individual will do the same. Indeed, the guiding principles are attitudinal benchmarks that enable you and others to assess progress toward acknowledging and valuing cultural differences, and while this assessment yields crucial information, it is insufficient by itself in provoking the development of culturally proficient behaviors.

In Table 3.1 (in the "Cultural Proficiency Matrices" section below), we use the guiding principles to provide a framework showing how the diversity of students informs professional practice in responding to student learning needs.

Barriers to Cultural Proficiency

The guiding principles provide a moral compass for culturally proficient actions, but there are often barriers to achieving culturally proficient actions. Resistance to change, systems of oppression, and a sense of entitlement militate against cultural proficiency. These barriers are often manifested in statements such as this: "It is not *me* that needs to change. I have been a successful educator for years; these kids/parents just need to get a clue!"

Similarly, it is rare to find a person who doesn't acknowledge that racism, ethnocentrism, and sexism exist in our society. What they often fail to see, however, is that when one group of people loses rights and privileges due to

Resistance to change, systems of oppression, and a sense of entitlement militate against cultural proficiency.

systemic oppression, those rights and privileges accrue to others in often unacknowledged or unrecognized ways. As discussed earlier in this chapter, it is when one recognizes one's entitlement that he or she has the ability to make choices that benefit the education of children and youth. The matrices that comprise the Cultural Proficiency Equity Audit provide illustrations of how one can use one's position as an educator to make beneficial choices.

The Continuum of Cultural Proficiency

The continuum is one of the two tools used to construct each of the matrices. Table 3.2 (Parent and Community Involvement) illustrates the two phases of the continuum. The first three points focus on *them* (i.e., Cultural Destructiveness, Cultural Incapacity, Cultural Blindness); the next three points of the continuum focus on our *practice* (i.e., Cultural Precompetence, Cultural Competence, Cultural Proficiency). The six points of the continuum are these:

- Cultural Destructiveness—Seeking to eliminate vestiges of the cultures of others
- Cultural Incapacity—Seeking to make the culture of others appear to be wrong
- Cultural Blindness—Refusing to acknowledge the culture of others
- Cultural Precompetence—Being aware of what one doesn't know about working in diverse settings. Initial levels of awareness after which a person/organization can move in a positive, constructive direction or they can falter, stop, and possibly regress
- Cultural Competence—Viewing one's personal and organizational work as an interactive arrangement in which the educator enters into diverse settings in a manner that is additive to cultures that are different from the educator's
- Cultural Proficiency—Making the commitment to lifelong learning for the purpose of being increasingly effective in serving the educational needs of cultural groups. Holding the vision of what can be and committing to assessments that serve as benchmarks on the road to student success

The Five Essential Elements of Cultural Competence

These elements are the second of the two tools used to construct each of the matrices. The essential elements become the standards for culturally competent values, behaviors, policies, and practices.

Closely examine Table 3.2 further below, taking particular note of the column titled Cultural Competence. Read down the column to see how the elements (i.e., standards) become the planning components for deep personal and organizational work.

- Assessing Cultural Knowledge—Being aware of what you know about others' cultures, how you react to others' cultures, and what you need to do to be effective in cross-cultural situations
- Valuing Diversity—Making the effort to include people whose viewpoints and experiences are different from yours and will enrich conversations, decision making, and problem solving
- Managing the Dynamics of Difference—Viewing conflict as a natural and normal process in human communication that has cultural contexts to be understood and used to support creative problem solving
- Adapting to Diversity—Having the will to learn about others and the ability to use others' cultural experiences and backgrounds in educational settings
- Institutionalizing Cultural Knowledge—Making learning about cultural groups and their experiences and perspectives an integral part of your ongoing learning

EVOLUTION OF THE CULTURAL PROFICIENCY EQUITY AUDIT

The concept and practice of the equity audit has evolved in response to the limitations of external audits. There have been two particularly troubling trends in education: the placing of low-income children and children of color into learning environments where the predominant focus is on

The Cultural Proficiency Equity Audit was devised as a means of providing educators with a tool designed to close the equity gap in achievement.

improving test scores; and the presence of peer and supervisory teams in classrooms and schools who are auditing classroom practices and materials. We don't argue against such practices as possibly a beginning point, but we are concerned that they are becoming institutionalized and that they can lead to a climate of mistrust, fear, anger, and, most importantly, a continued ignoring of the complex needs of our children and youth.

The Cultural Proficiency Equity Audit was devised as a means of providing educators with a tool designed to close the equity gap in achievement. When the achievement gap is framed as an equity gap, responsibility moves from testing students to determining if they are failing/succeeding to using test scores as one indicator that leads us to examine our practices as teachers, counselors, and administrators. The Cultural Proficiency Equity Audit is a set of four matrices: Curriculum and Instruction, Assessment and Accountability, Parents and Community, and Professional Development.

CONDUCTING A CULTURALLY PROFICIENT EQUITY AUDIT

For the past decade or so, school reformers have discussed school change in terms of leverage points for change (Fullan, 2003; DuFour, DuFour, Eaker, & Karhanek, 2004; DuFour, Eaker, & DuFour, 2005; Kegan & Lahey, 2001; Reeves, 2000; Senge, 2005; Senge et al., 2000). Leverage points are the policies and practices over which educators have the most direct impact. Prominent leverage points for changing school practices are curriculum, instruction, contact with parents/community members, professional development, and the use of assessment data. Each of these leverage points provides educators with specific opportunities to shape the education of our students.

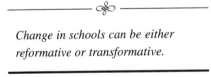

Change in schools can be either reformative or transformative.

Change in schools can be either reformative or transformative. Often, reform initiatives driven by external forces (e.g., No Child Left Behind) result in change processes that are compliance driven. Challenging one's own assumptions about who is being served by our schools, on the other hand, drives deeper, transformative initiatives (Argyris, 1990; Fullan, 2003; Hilliard, 1991; Schein, 1989). Educators who examine and challenge their own assumptions are prepared to challenge the system in such a manner that schools can be transformed to serve all students. It is the transformative approach to system change that brings together individual educators' moral commitment to developing schools that continue the unfolding of the democracy in this country.

In our forthcoming book, *Culturally Proficient Audits: Accountability for Educational Equity* (Lindsey, Graham, Westphal, & Jew, in press), we provide examples from our work with P–16 educators, organized into matrices and associated tools, to focus on how people transform their practices as administrators, teachers, and counselors in ways that serve the academic and social needs of their students. The four matrices currently under development are Curriculum and Instruction, Assessment and Accountability, Professional Development, and Parent and Community Involvement. For purposes of illustration, the Parent and Community Involvement matrix is presented later in this chapter.

The Culturally Proficient Equity Audit is intended to provide educators with a perspective of their policies and practices *in use*. The matrices provide concrete examples of the assumptions that either facilitate or hinder change. When educators accurately identify the assumptions that guide their work, and combine them with test data, they have guidelines for changing professional values, behavior, polices, and practices in ways that benefit historically underserved learners. Fundamental to personal transformation is learning to mediate one's own learning (i.e., change) as well as the learning of colleagues.

Key Components of a Culturally Proficient Equity Audit

The expected outcomes of conducting a Cultural Proficiency Equity Audit are to

- Examine the system and microsystems for equitable access and opportunities for all students
- Create a common language and vision for equity
- Develop plans for using equitable practices in closing achievement gaps
- Hold *courageous conversations* about the purpose of schooling in a democratic society and the imperative of educating all children and youth in our country
- Provide a framework for ongoing data collection, data analysis, and identification of findings that can lead to the development of educational improvement plans designed to reduce the achievement gap in schools

CULTURAL PROFICIENCY MATRICES

In developing the matrices, our first step was to operationally define each of the leverage points in the context of each of the essential elements of cultural competence. Table 3.1 presents the four leverage points (Curriculum and Instruction, Assessment, Parents and Community, and Professional Development), along with the five essential elements (Assessing Cultural Knowledge, Valuing Diversity, Managing the Dynamics of Difference, Adapting to Diversity, and Institutionalizing Cultural Knowledge).

Table 3.2 presents the Parents and Community Matrix. The other matrices are under development. When you read the descriptions under the Parents and Community column in Table 3.1, you will notice that the descriptions are imported into the first column of Table 3.2. The next section provides guidance in how to read the matrix.

Guide for Reading the Parents and Community Matrix for Culturally Proficient Equity Audits

Table 3.2 is the Parents and Community Matrix, which has the following characteristics:

The matrix is composed of rows and columns.

- Each of the rows is one of the five standards referred to as *essential elements of cultural competence.*
- There are seven columns. At the top of the first column is the title "Essential Elements." A brief description of the element is given in the context of the topic, parents and community.
- Each of the next six columns is one of the six points of the *cultural proficiency continuum.*
- The fifth column is titled "Cultural Competence." Each of the descriptors in that column describes one of the essential elements of cultural competence. The language is in active voice and describes actions that can be taken today in schools.
- The sixth column is titled "Cultural Proficiency." The description is future focused and measurable.

Now reflect on your own decoding of the matrix. What are ways in which you might able to use this tool in your professional practice?

Table 3.1 Operational Definitions—Leverage Points' Intersection With Essential Elements

| Five Essential Elements | Curriculum and Instruction (C & I) | Leverage Points | | |
		Assessment	Parents and Community	Professional Development
Assessing Cultural Knowledge	Extent to which C & I provides opportunities for educators and students to learn about and respect one's own and others' cultures	Extent to which disaggregated data are used to enhance knowledge about cultural groups	Extent to which community involvement facilitates cultural identity development and sharing cultural knowledge	Extent to which professional development promotes and facilitates cultural identity development and sharing of cultural knowledge
Valuing Diversity	Extent to which C & I reflects diversity	Extent to which data and data-driven decisions reflect cultural differences	Extent to which parent and community diversity and input is valued	Extent to which professional development integrates cultural diversity and equity issues
Managing the Dynamics of Difference	Extent to which C & I accommodates diverse learners, promotes multiple perspectives and social justice	Extent to which data are used to identify access, learning, and achievement gaps between cultural groups	Extent to which parents, community, and staff develop capacity to promote and support multiple perspectives and mediate cultural conflict between and among diverse parent/community groups and the school	Extent to which professional development promotes and models the use of inquiry and dialogue to promote multiple perspectives and mediate conflict that may arise

(Continued)

Table 3.1 (Continued)

Five Essential Elements	Leverage Points			
	Curriculum and Instruction (C & I)	Assessment	Parents and Community	Professional Development
Adapting to Diversity	Extent to which core curriculum and instructional program integrate cultural knowledge and ability of diverse student groups	Extent to which data shape practices to meet the needs of cultural groups and close gaps	Extent to which parent/community/staff groups shift and develop values and approaches to support and promote diverse group needs	Extent to which professional learning facilitates personal and organizational changes to meet the diverse needs of the community
Institutionalizing Cultural Knowledge	Extent to which culturally responsive C & I is supported and promoted by community and staff values and organizational policies and practices	Extent to which assessment data shape community and staff values, policies, practices, and structures to meet the needs of cultural groups, and close access, learning, and achievement gaps, thereby ensuring educational equity systemwide	Extent to which parents/community/staff integrate cultural knowledge into organization's policies/practices and structures to meet diverse group needs	Extent to which professional development shapes policies, practices. and structures that meet the needs of the present and future diverse community

Table 3.2 Parent and Community Involvement

5 Essential Elements	Cultural Destructiveness	Cultural Incapacity	Cultural Blindness	Cultural Precompetence	Cultural Competence	Cultural Proficiency
Assessing Cultural Knowledge Extent to which community involvement facilitates the development of cultural identity and sharing cultural knowledge	Ignore, intimidate, or punish the expression of needs of diverse parent/community groups.	Help culturally diverse parent and community members by purposefully assimilating them into the dominant culture.	Promote and support parent, community, and school leaders, agendas, and initiatives without acknowledging the needs of diverse cultural groups.	Recognizing the importance of knowing about each other's cultures, parent, community, and school leaders may learn about each other in inauthentic ways.	Learn about each others' cultures in authentic ways in order to bridge the gaps between and among home, community, and school cultures.	All stakeholders continuously scan the environment in order to respond to ever-changing community demographics and raise awareness about future demographic trends.
Valuing Diversity Extent to which parent and community diversity and input are valued	Actively prevent involvement of diverse cultural groups in making decisions about programs and services that meet the needs of all students.	Identify cultural differences of parents and community groups as deficiencies and implement strategies to remediate such deficiencies.	Respond to legal mandates for parent and community involvement without regard for actual needs of diverse cultural groups.	Recognizing need to involve culturally diverse community groups in decision making, diverse groups or their representatives may be included in limiting or inappropriate ways.	Involve representative parents and community members as partners in making decisions about programs and services that meet the needs of all students.	All stakeholders advocate for closing gaps and achieving equitable outcomes and social justice for all cultural groups.

(Continued)

Table 3.2 (Continued)

5 Essential Elements	Cultural Destructiveness	Cultural Incapacity	Cultural Blindness	Cultural Precompetence	Cultural Competence	Cultural Proficiency
Managing the Dynamics of Difference Extent to which parents, community, and staff develop capacity to promote and support multiple perspectives and mediate cultural conflict between and among diverse parent/community groups and the school	Limit or intimidate involvement of some parent and community groups by allocating resources inequitably and promoting agendas of dominant groups over other groups' needs.	Ignore and/or suppress parent and community groups that are working to address issues important to them.	Facilitate groups working together to find common ground on divisive issues.	Recognizing the possibility for emerging intergroup conflict, parents, community, and staff may develop conflict-resolution strategies or identify *key liaisons* within diverse cultural groups to manage the dynamics within those groups.	Create a culture that encourages multiple perspectives and builds capacity for and practices dialogue between and among all community, parent, and school groups.	All stakeholders work together to anticipate and raise awareness about the needs of the ever-changing community.
Adapting to Diversity Extent to which parents, community, and staff shift and develop values	Prevent approaches or adaptations intended to benefit parents/ community and student groups	Limit or resist approaches/ adaptations intended to meet the needs of culturally diverse groups	Parents, community, and school staff groups do not acknowledge or adapt to meet the needs of	Recognizing differences between home and school cultures, parents, community, and staff begin to address needs of diverse	Work together to identify needs of diverse cultural populations, often adapting current practices to meet such needs.	All stakeholders work together to develop values, capacity, and advocacy for creating and maintaining an

(Continued)

Table 3.2 (Continued)

5 Essential Elements	Cultural Destructiveness	Cultural Incapacity	Cultural Blindness	Cultural Precompetence	Cultural Competence	Cultural Proficiency
and approaches to support and promote diverse group needs		because such adaptations are seen as divisive and against the common good.	culturally diverse community groups.	populations, sometimes in limited or inappropriate ways.		infrastructure that responds to the needs of a diverse community.
Institutionalizing Extent to which parents, community, and staff integrate cultural knowledge into organizations policies, practices, and structures to meet diverse group needs	Create policies and practices that systematically exclude *culturally different* parent groups from being involved in important decisions about the education of their children.	Maintain status quo and policies/practices that support dominant group needs and hasten the assimilation *of different* cultural groups.	Maintain policies, practices, and structures that support traditional parent and community organizations, and involvement, believing that such policies and practices serve all cultural groups equally well.	Recognizing diverse community needs as they arise, parents, community, and school staff may develop policies, procedures, and structures to respond to diverse needs in limited or inappropriate ways, often containing and isolating the needs of diverse community groups on ad hoc committees.	Develop policies and practices and create structures that address the diverse cultural needs of parent, community, and student groups, and assess effectiveness in meeting those needs and closing gaps between groups.	All stakeholders develop and maintain channels for communication and decision making that ensure ongoing meaningful contributions and input from diverse community groups to school/district policies and practices.

In Closing

The theme of this volume, "engaging *every* learner," is a noble direction for a profession and a country that profess the highest democratic ideals. Although both our country and our profession have an equity-resistant history, our democratic ideals have provided us the opportunity to develop tools to overcome the inequities fostered by systems of oppression and the concomitant systems of privilege that persist in our schools and society. The matrices for Culturally Proficient Equity Audits are one tool for use by educators who commit themselves to closing the academic achievement gap.

References

Argyris, C. (1990). *Overcoming organizational defenses: Facilitating organizational learning.* Englewood Cliffs, NJ: Prentice Hall.

Carter, T., P. (1970). *Mexican Americans in school: A history of educational neglect.* New York: College Entrance Examination Board.

Cross, T., Bazron, B., Dennis, K., & Isaacs, M. (1989). *Toward a culturally competent system of care* (Vol. 1). Washington, DC: Georgetown University Child Development Program, Child and Adolescent Service System Program.

Douglass, F. (1960). *The narrative of the life of Frederick Douglass: An American slave.* Cambridge, MA: Belknap Press.

DuFour, R., DuFour, R., Eaker, R., & Karhanek, G. (2004). *Whatever it takes: How professional learning communities respond when kids don't learn.* Bloomington, IN: National Educational Service.

DuFour, R., Eaker, R., & DuFour, R. (2005). *On common ground: The power of professional learning communities.* Bloomington, IN: National Educational Service.

Ellison, R. (1952). *Invisible man.* New York: Random House.

Fullan, M. (2003). *The moral imperative of school leadership.* Thousand Oaks, CA: Corwin Press.

Haycock, K., Jerald, C., & Huang, S. (2001). *Closing the gap: Done in a decade.* Washington, DC: The Education Trust.

Hilliard, A. (1991). Do we have the will to educate all children? *Educational Leadership, 40*(1), 31–36.

Kegan, R., & Lahey, L. (2001). *How the way we talk can change the way we work: Seven languages for transformation.* San Francisco: Jossey-Bass.

Lindsey, R. B., Graham, S., Westphal Jr., C., & Jew, C. (in press). *Culturally proficient audits: Accountability for educational equity.* Thousand Oaks, CA.: Corwin Press.

Lindsey, R. B., Nuri Robins, K., & Terrell, R. D. (2003). *Cultural proficiency: A manual for school leaders* (2nd ed.). Thousand Oaks, CA: Corwin Press.

No Child Left Behind Act. (2001). Available: http://www.ed.gov/nclb

Nuri Robins, K., Lindsey, R. B., Lindsey, D. B., & Terrell, R. D. (2006). *Culturally proficient instruction: A guide for people who teach* (2nd ed.). Thousand Oaks, CA: Corwin Press.

Perie, M., Moran, R., Lutkus, A. D., & Tirre, W. (2005). *NAEP 2004 trends in academic progress: Three decades of student performance in reading and mathematics* (NCES 2005–464). Washington, DC: National Center for Education Statistics.

Quality counts at 10: A decade of standards-based education. (2006, January 5). *Education Week, 25*(17).

Reeves, D. B. (2000). *Accountability in action: A blueprint for learning organizations.* Denver, CO: Center for Performance Assessment.

Schein, E. (1989). *Organizational culture and leadership: A dynamic view.* San Francisco: Jossey-Bass.

Senge, P., Cambron, N. H., McCabe, T. L., Kleiner, A., Dutton, J., & Smith, B. (2000). *Schools that learn: A fifth discipline fieldbook for educators, parents, and everyone who cares about education.* New York: Doubleday.

Senge, P., Kleiner, A., Roberts, C., Roth, G., Ross, R. B., & Smith, B. S. (1999). *The dance of change.* New York: Doubleday.

Snyder, T. D. (2005). *Digest of educational statistics 2005.* Washington, DC: U.S. Department of Education, Office of Educational Research and Improvement.

Starnes, B. A. (2006). What we don't know can hurt them: White teachers, Indian children. *Phi Delta Kappan, 87*(5), 384–392.

Stiggins, R. (2005). From formative assessment to assessment for learning: A path to success in standards-based schools. *Phi Delta Kappan, 87*(4).

Takaki, R. (1993). *A different mirror: A history of multicultural America.* Boston: Little, Brown.

Wartell, M. A., & Huelskamp, R. M. (1991, July 18). *Testimony of Michael A. Wartell and Robert M. Huelskamp, Sandia National Laboratories, before the Subcommittee on Elementary, Secondary, and Vocational Education, Committee on Education and Labor, U.S. House of Representatives.*

CHAPTER FOUR

THE EMERGENCE OF A KNOWLEDGE BASE FOR TEACHING DIVERSE LEARNERS IN BIG-CITY SCHOOLS

From Practice to Theory to Practice

ANTOINETTE MITCHELL

The historic purposes of the American public school system include nurturing intellectual growth, developing civic consciousness, and encouraging the social development of the nation's youth.[1] Two additional vitally important purposes include the custodial function of keeping youth constructively occupied and the economic imperative to prepare the next generation for future employment. During the 20th century, schools repeatedly fell short of these lofty goals, particularly schools in urban areas that serve poor children and children of color. The predictable response to this failure has always been some attempt at school reform (Tyack, 1990). Yet the seemingly intractable problems remain.

Teachers and administrators in urban schools are often criticized because of their inability to educate everybody's children. Expectations for what it means to educate a child have changed greatly over the past century, as the U.S. economy has moved from agrarian, to industrial, to service, and now, increasingly, to a global setting. Expectations have moved from increasing literacy, to understanding the basic skills, to a more intense emphasis on math and science education, to teaching higher-order skills such as communication, computation, analysis, and critical thinking (Cuban & Usdan, 2003; Reich, 1992). Some contend that the most important skill students need to learn for the 21st century is "how to learn," and they maintain that universal post-secondary education is an imperative (Friedman, 2005). Still others simply hope to see the achievement gap between children of color and their white middle-class peers decrease.

The year 2004 marked the 50th anniversary of the *Brown v. Board of Education* decision. A report by the National Commission on Teaching and America's Future (NCTAF) published the same year included the following:

> As we mark the fiftieth anniversary of the *Brown v. Board of Education* decision, millions of low income and children of color are concentrated in separate and unequal schools. Many are being taught by unqualified teachers, with insufficient instructional materials and a limited supply of textbooks and inadequate technology, in crumbling buildings—with vermin and broken bathrooms. These substandard teaching and learning conditions are rarely found in schools where the majority of students come from more affluent homes and have a low risk of school failure. We have a two-tiered education system. (NCTAF, 2004)

This two-tiered education system—one predominantly white and middle class, and the other predominantly of color and poor—is at the heart of the problem we face (Kozol, 1991, 1995). According to David Berliner (2005), poverty is the 800-pound gorilla that nobody wants to talk about, but is nonetheless a causal factor in the failure of schools to educate all children. After detailing how environmental factors caused by poverty (such as inadequate health care, a declining number of positive role models in neighborhoods, and lack of academic stimulation during the summer) affect academic achievement, Berliner contends that there are solutions to this problem that exist *beyond* the educational context and solutions that are *within* the educational context. Both sets of solutions are important if we are truly to commit ourselves to educating everybody's children.

Poverty is the 800-pound gorilla that nobody wants to talk about, but it is a causal factor in the failure of schools to educate all children (Berliner, 2005).

While Berliner describes several out-of-school actions that we as a society can take to eliminate poverty and thus address the low academic achievement of urban students, I shall concentrate on the in-school solutions, or those that exist within the educational context. First, I'll detail the roles played by those teachers who are successful with urban students. This section draws on oral-history interviews conducted with retired urban school teachers who were deemed outstanding by principals, peers, students, and parents. Using their philosophies and behaviors as a springboard for understanding teacher knowledge in the urban context, I shall then turn to teacher education, particularly the recent emergence of a codified body of knowledge for the preparation of practitioners who can work effectively with students from diverse socioeconomic and cultural backgrounds. The next section addresses why it is important for all teachers to be exposed to and learn this emergent body of knowledge by drawing on a concept called "thin-slicing," or rapid cognition. Finally, I will discuss how the National Council for Accreditation of Teacher Education is working with 700 schools, colleges, and departments of education (SCDEs) to help produce teachers who can be successful with all students.

The Wisdom of Practice

The quality of the teacher is the most important in-school variable that explains variation in student achievement (Fetler, 1999; NCTAF, 1996; Wenglinsky, 2002). While some speak of quality in terms of content-area major, level and type of teacher preparation, and type of certification, here I am more interested in what characterizes the teaching of those practitioners who are effective with low-income, urban students. To address the issue of teacher characteristics, I draw on the findings in the literature on teachers who are effective with urban students and on a historical study based on oral-history interviews with eight retired teachers who worked in the Washington, DC, public schools between 1960 and 1990 (Mitchell, 1996). Though the urban context changed and educational fads came and went, the themes remained constant. Throughout this section, I include quotes from several of the teachers to illustrate some of the themes cited.

Educational literature suggests that teachers who are effective with urban students are adept at using culturally relevant or culturally responsive pedagogy. This type of pedagogy draws on the cultural background of the students to motivate them, to help them learn, and to positively affect their self-concept and attitudes (Irvine, 2003). A critical component of culturally relevant pedagogy is that the teachers genuinely care about their students and their students' academic and social development.

A critical component of culturally relevant pedagogy is that the teachers genuinely care about their students and their students' academic and social development.

When translated into action, practicing culturally relevant pedagogy means that effective teachers play several important roles in the lives of students, including the roles of cultural mediator, advocate, and supporter of student growth and development (Mitchell, 2000).

As cultural mediators, for instance, teachers must have a two-pronged philosophical understanding. On one hand, they acknowledge the strengths and challenges in their students' backgrounds and value the dignity and perseverance found in urban communities. They know and share the belief in education as a means of social and economic uplift. Further, they understand and appreciate the current and historical effects of racism, segregation, and poverty on student growth and development. They understand how poverty and other outside-of-school problems associated with unemployment and underemployment adversely affect student growth and development.

On the other hand, teachers who are effective with urban students also understand that their students are children who can learn at high levels, who are curious about the world around them, and who will acquire knowledge and skills when taught appropriately. As cultural mediators, teachers anchor their understanding of and behavior toward students in the reality of the students' lived experiences and in the possibilities of the students' potential as learners. Effective teachers understand that often, when students behave in a nonproductive manner, the behaviors are the symptoms of larger problems in students' lives.

Good teachers attempt to help students learn despite these larger problems. Such teachers strike an important balance between recognizing social forces that contribute to student attitudes and behaviors and recognizing students as individuals who, through individual agency, are able to make independent choices based on a logical assessment of the consequences. Through providing advice, sharing information with other teachers, giving students support and encouragement, and occasionally providing lunch money or a token for transportation, the teachers play an active role in the lives of the students—understanding the complexity of student behavior and attempting to mediate between the needs of home and school. One teacher mused,

> I believe that students want to learn. They don't come to school necessarily to cause problems. They may have a lot of things going on in their lives that come out as disruptive in the learning situation, but basically students want to learn.

Another teacher said,

> I think the worse things got around them, the more children needed guidance. They really did. They needed people to talk to them about where they were in all of this and where they were going, and if they had a future in all of this. This is what we tried—I tried—to do with them. Talk to them, keep them going. Let them see that there was something ahead for them.

Effective teachers also mediate between the home and school through their work with parents. These teachers consider the parent–teacher relationship important because it has the potential to significantly increase student achievement through its impact on student behavior and attitudes. Culturally responsive teachers are able to foster positive relationships with parents through proactive engagement. The teachers recognize that parenting is hard work for everyone, but especially for lower-income, often single parents and family members. They realize that students' families may not be able or even willing to physically come to the school, but that these families care about their children and their children's education. The teachers contact parents through telephone calls, notes, and home visits. They share what is happening in their classes and ask parents if they have questions. They inform parents about upcoming events and invite parents to participate. According to one teacher,

> See, I was one who would call the [parents]. We talked about everything. I would always let the parents know. I . . . would tell them what we were going to do. I would send home things. I had a lot of cooperation with my parents because I would try to clue them in on the things we were doing. When we started taking field trips, they would go along with me, a lot of them.

Ultimately, they establish a respectful, informative, and ongoing relationship with parents. If it is necessary to talk with parents about problems with student behavior or academic performance, it is done in the context of this supportive, nurturing relationship.

This proactive approach to parental involvement is very much in line with current research on family-school partnerships, which encourage schools to take the initiative in fostering collaborative relationships (Epstein et al., 2002). The collaborative relationships provide support for students and the opportunity for teachers to learn about families' strengths and challenges and to develop interpersonal relationships that can be used to bridge gaps created by class, gender, race, and age. In this context, the teachers are playing the role of mediator between home and school.

Another role played by teachers who are effective with urban youth is that of advocate. In this role, teachers participate in activities designed to support student learning that may be outside of the classroom. Teachers attend meetings of the Board of Education and other policy boards to discuss the quality and quantity of textbooks available to them. One teacher recalled appearing before the school district's Board of Education:

> I was always one to go to board meetings. I would go sometimes as a representative of the PTA and sometimes just as a teacher. I complained about the books, the lack of books or about how old they were. Sometimes I felt that the content was ridiculously easy and I complained about that, too. The kids were getting shortchanged and I want[ed] to make some noise, see what could be done.

These teachers encourage principals and other administrators to make improvements in school buildings, to supply them with adequate teaching resources, and to provide personnel skilled in specialty areas. Effective teachers engage in constructive discussions with their peers, sharing information and teaching strategies that help them to work better with the students. Further, effective teachers are good at recognizing when problems are beyond their roles. They understand the work of other school professionals such as social workers, school psychologists, counselors, and special educators. They know when and how to make use of these resources when they are available.

Finally, effective teachers play the role of instructor, helping students achieve academically. Good teachers know their field well and have an in-depth knowledge of how to teach it. They are able to teach using multiple strate-

Effective teachers believe strongly in students' innate ability to learn and that it is their responsibility to ensure that learning takes place.

gies and perspectives. They use formative assessments to discover where students are and what students know and work from there. As one teacher recalls,

> In the classroom, you have to roll with the punches. You make the adjustments. You get your students in and you find out where they are. You know you better get down there where they are in order to bring them up. So you just tell them your expectations. Your expectations are high. And you motivate them. You have to say, "I know you can do well."

Significantly, effective teachers believe strongly in the students' innate ability to learn and that it is their responsibility to ensure that learning takes place. The teachers manifest this belief by maintaining high expectations for students and creating classroom situations in which students feel comfortable and nurtured. One teacher illustrated this when she said,

> Different people see different things in children. I see that they're eager to learn. They're going to carry on a whole lot of foolishness before they get down to business, but when you really start with those children, they want to learn. And they are great learners, great learners.

Effective teachers view their work with students in a context larger than academic achievement. They recognize the importance of helping students think critically about the world and their place in it. They recognize the motivating effect of relating what is taught to the students' experiences, interests, and goals. Effective teachers realize that they are engaged in the business of shaping lives. They are not only teaching social studies, but also what it means to live and participate in a democratic society. They are not only teaching skills needed for employment, but also the possibilities for careers that many students may never have dreamed of. They are not only teaching how to write a paper, but also how to access and process information. They work not only to help students pass from one grade to the next, but also to encourage students to finish high school and go to college. Effective teachers are acutely aware of the fact that they play a multiplicity of roles in students' lives; they believe that their work, when done well, will positively affect the students' growth and development long after the students have left their classrooms. According to one teacher,

> [Students] need extra encouragement and friendship; they also need discipline to help them make the right decisions. Education is giving students the tools to make the right decisions. Ultimately, the decisions are theirs to make, but if they have the foundation, they usually end up doing what is in their own best interest. And I think that's what being a teacher is all about.

Ultimately, effective teachers care about the life chances of their students. They understand that socioeconomic factors pose barriers to achievement, and they work in the affective domain to help students be resilient and move beyond these barriers. Research suggests that resiliency is fostered by caring and supportive relationships, positive and high expectations, and opportunities for meaningful participation. Through their beliefs and behaviors, effective teachers work to promote resiliency in students and view academic achievement as an important part of this process.

Effective teachers view their work with students in a context larger than academic achievement.

Through these behaviors and beliefs, tried and tempered in the forge of the everyday classroom, the best teachers have learned methods and techniques for succeeding with urban students. These behaviors and beliefs, this culturally responsive pedagogy, constitute the wisdom of practice (Ladson-Billings, 1994; Nieto, 2003; Villegas & Lucas, 2002). Many of the tenets of this approach—including the importance of caring (Noddings, 1992), the importance of understanding and involving the school community (Comer, 1980), and an emphasis on the relevance of family and community involvement (Epstein et al., 2002)—are corroborated by research.

We watch the best urban teachers use their hard-won wisdom, day after day, to change the lives and the futures of urban youth.

To summarize, we can watch the best urban teachers use their hard-won wisdom, day after day, to change the lives and the futures of urban youth. Moreover, we find their practical wisdom echoed in the professional literature. Let us now examine the implications of this congruence for the preparation of teachers.

PREPARATION FOR EFFECTIVENESS

For educators in the policy arena, a critical question is this: Is being an effective teacher—one who embodies the behaviors and beliefs of culturally responsive pedagogy—something that is innate, or is it something that can be taught and learned? Many researchers, practitioners, and educational policy makers seem to be reaching agreement on a core body of knowledge that is considered important for all teachers to know in order to be effective with all students—including students of color, poor students, and English language learners. This emergent knowledge base includes many of the elements listed above, such as knowledge in the content area, professional knowledge and skills, an understanding of and respect for the role of diversity in teaching and learning, and a commitment to helping all students learn.

The National Academy of Education (NAE), founded in 1965, is an honorary society of highly respected educational researchers. A few years ago, the NAE sponsored a blue-ribbon committee to study the knowledge and skills that teachers need to know in order to help children learn and develop. The work of this committee culminated in two books: *Preparing Teachers for a Changing World* (Darling-Hammond & Bransford, 2005), which provided the research base for the second book, *A Good Teacher in Every*

Classroom: Preparing the Highly Qualified Teachers Our Children Deserve (Darling-Hammond & Snowden, 2005).

Together, these works codify a knowledge base for teacher preparation that is founded on an analysis of current research in learning, teaching, and teacher education. According to this research, in order to be able to work successfully with all students, including students of color and students who are poor, teachers need to

- Know their subject well and know how to teach it to students
- Understand how children learn and develop
- Be able to observe, monitor, and assess children to gain accurate feedback about their learning and development
- Know themselves—understand their own language and culture and know how to learn about other cultures with different language patterns and ways of knowing
- Be able to develop a curriculum and learning activities that connect what they know about their students to what the students need to learn
- Know how to teach specific subject matter in ways that are accessible, anticipating and addressing student conceptions and misconceptions
- Know how to develop and use assessments that measure learning standards and how to use the results to plan teaching that will address student learning needs
- Know how to use systematic inquiry, including how to observe an individual child in interaction with different tasks and other students to diagnose his or her needs
- Be able to evaluate why children may be responding or behaving in particular ways given the context of the classroom, the individual nature of the learning challenges, and the child's life outside of school
- Be able to develop interventions, track changes, and revise their instructional strategies as necessary (Darling-Hammond & Snowden, 2005, pp. 27–28)

For the detailed description of what teachers need to know about how children learn, the committee drew on a work sponsored by the National Research Council titled *How People Learn: Brain, Mind, Experiences, and School* (Bransford, Brown, & Cockling, 1999). Four findings from this work—deemed by the committee to be critical components of the knowledge base for teachers—are the following:

- The constructive nature of knowing—the fact that we all actively attempt to interpret our world based on our existing skills, knowledge, and developmental levels. This means that teachers need to understand what students already know and believe and be able to build bridges between students' prior experience and new knowledge. This includes anticipating student misunderstandings in particular areas so that they can be addressed.
- Cognitive processing—how people attend to, perceive, and process information; retain it in short- and long-term memory; and retrieve it. This includes understanding the importance of organizing information so that it can be connected to other ideas, incorporated into a schema for learning new information, and retrieved when needed.
- Metacognition—how people learn to monitor and regulate their own learning and thinking. This includes knowing how to teach students to think about what they understand, what they need to learn, and what strategies they can use to acquire the information they need.
- Motivation—what encourages students to become and remain engaged with their learning. This includes knowing what kinds of tasks, supports, and feedback encourage students to put forth effort and strive to improve. (Darling-Hammond & Snowden, 2005, p. 8)

In addition to knowing how to assess student learning using formative assessments, as well as knowing how to manage a classroom by creating a supportive environment with shared expectations for learning, the emergent knowledge base further indicates that beginning teachers should know how to work with students from diverse backgrounds and students with learning differences. As the population of public schools grows increasingly diverse, new teachers are best equipped to help all students learn when they are able to connect with what students already know, when they understand how students are socialized, and when they have knowledge about student experiences outside of school. The knowledge base suggests that it is important that beginning teachers learn about students'

Beginning teachers should know how to work with students from diverse backgrounds and students with learning differences.

families and communities so that they can motivate and engage students and encourage family involvement in schooling. The knowledge base also suggests that teachers can "help mediate the boundary crossings that many students must manage between home and school" (Darling-Hammond & Snowden, 2005, p. 21).

Given that today's classrooms include many students with exceptionalities, some recognized and some not, the emergent knowledge base recognizes that teachers also need to know how to help students who learn differently. They need a working knowledge of the most common disabilities, such as dyslexia, developmental delays, autism, and attention deficit disorder. They should know how to make adaptations related to the time it takes to complete tasks, the level of difficulty, and the kinds of assistance to offer. They need to understand their roles and responsibilities as they relate to special education.

Taken together, the knowledge, skills, and behaviors outlined above represent the most current thinking on the preparation of effective educators. The knowledge, skills, and behaviors are translated into effectiveness through practice. It is the job of formal teacher education to expose teacher candidates to the emergent knowledge base while providing context that will enable them to move from theory to practice.

But might it be possible that this imposing catalogue of knowledge, skills, and behaviors is more theoretical than useful? Indeed, some have argued that professional knowledge in teaching is unnecessary and has limited impact on student learning. However, proponents of this view overlook an elusive but important element of teaching: decision making. That vitally important element is the subject of the following section.

THIN-SLICING AND TEACHER EDUCATION

Some people believe that many of the decisions we make—especially those decisions we make quickly—are the result of intuition. In a recent book titled *Blink*, Malcolm Gladwell (2005) posits that many decisions that are made quickly are actually the result of sophisticated subconscious processing called rapid cognition, or "thin-slicing." Thin-slicing is the ability to draw on a knowledge and experiential base to sift through information for what is important, to see patterns that may not be obvious, and to identify significant relationships. In the professional realm, these abilities enable experts to make good decisions and solve difficult problems with great rapidity.

Teachers are believed to make countless thousands of decisions each day as they work with students, colleagues, and families. They make decisions about how to shape the context of their classrooms, how to build trust with students, and how to respond to student attitudes, beliefs, and behaviors. They decide what to include in their lesson plans, what pedagogical approaches to take, how to assess

Teachers are believed to make countless thousands of decisions each day as they work with students, colleagues, and families.

student learning, and how to adapt instruction. They make decisions about the content and tone of their interactions with colleagues. They decide how to approach their students' families, how often they interact with families, and what the nature of that interaction will be. *Teachers who are effective with all students are experts who thin-slice all the time.* Many of their decisions are made very quickly, seemingly intuitively. In truth, they, like the professionals in Gladwell's book, are drawing on their experiences and preexisting knowledge to guide them in their decision making.

According to Cochran-Smith and Fries (2005), some researchers believe that "teachers' knowledge frames and belief structures are the filters through which teachers' practices, strategies, actions, interpretations and decisions are made." Consequently, teachers' knowledge frames and belief structures affect their practice and indirectly affect student growth and development. It seems that teachers who are most effective with urban students from culturally and socioeconomically diverse backgrounds are those who have knowledge frames and belief structures that are aligned with the dictates of culturally relevant pedagogy and other aspects of the emergent knowledge base described above.

Based on studying the expertise of different professionals, Gladwell further posits that the ability to thin-slice can be "educated" or shaped by the introduction of new knowledge and experiences. This leads to two important implications for teacher education. First, it suggests that preservice teachers need to learn the knowledge and skills that make up the emergent knowledge base in order to become fully effective educators whose decisions are shaped by the standards of the profession. Second, given that most teacher education students are white females with limited experiences with cultural diversity, teacher education programs must continue to work toward providing teacher candidates with learning experiences in diverse P–12 settings. These experiences, when properly structured, can raise awareness levels (Hollins & Guzman, 2005) and create a more enabling experiential base.

If this emergent knowledge base for teachers is grounded in research on learning and teaching, includes the wisdom of practice, and focuses on P–12 student learning, then another important policy question is this: How do we as a nation ensure that teachers are systematically exposed to this emerging knowledge base? Traditionally, teachers are exposed to new information through preservice and inservice learning. This method requires information to trickle down through the numerous state and district professional development activities and through individual teacher preparation programs. Another rather nontraditional way to ensure that most teachers are exposed to this emergent knowledge base is through the avenue of accreditation of teacher education programs, where most new teachers are prepared and where most current teachers seek continuing education.

THE INFLUENCE OF NCATE

The organization most closely associated with accreditation in teacher education is the National Council for Accreditation of Teacher Education (NCATE). Founded in 1954, NCATE has long sought to bring about consensus within the educational community on standards for the preparation of educators. The organization's governance structure consists of quadrants representing practitioners, teacher educators, state and national policy makers, and specialized professional organizations. NCATE's governing boards are made up of representatives from each quadrant who are nominated by NCATE's 33 constituent members.[2] NCATE has partnerships with 48 states (and two territories) and is working with one of two major testing companies to align its standards with state licensing exams. Currently, NCATE accredits 612 of the 1,200 schools of education in the United States and has another 100 institutions in the accreditation pipeline. NCATE institutions graduate two-thirds of the new teachers produced each year. It is an organization that works with a broad spectrum of the education community and forges consensus around the development and implementation of standards for teacher education.

NCATE is also an organization that is dedicated to helping schools, colleges, and departments of education prepare teachers who can work effectively with all students. NCATE accreditation is a rigorous review of the educator preparation programs within an institution based on the national standards and guided by a philosophical orientation of teaching as a profession with an emergent knowledge base that is informed by research and the wisdom of practice.

NCATE is dedicated to helping schools, colleges, and departments of education prepare teachers who can work effectively with all students.

In fall 2001, NCATE introduced performance-based accreditation and a set of revised accreditation standards. Performance-based accreditation relies more on assessment data collected on what teacher candidates know and are able to do and less on traditional inputs like course requirements and faculty resumes. The new standards, known as the NCATE Unit Standards (NCATE, 2002), are used in conjunction with sets of discipline-specific standards to determine whether or not institutions have high-quality programs that prepare teacher candidates to work successfully with all students. Four of the six NCATE unit standards are described below.[3]

- Standard 1 identifies the knowledge, skills, and professional dispositions expected of preservice educators. It includes content knowledge; pedagogical knowledge and skills; professional knowledge including child development, educational foundations, and theories related to learning; and the ability to effect and assess the learning of all students.

- Standard 2 describes the assessment system that institutions must develop and maintain to track candidate learning and the operation of the program. In addition to candidate assessment, the system must also collect data from graduates and employers on the quality of the programs. The standard also requires institutions to make improvements to courses and programs based on the data.

- Standard 3 requires that institutions ensure that candidates have experiences in school settings that gradually lead to a clinical experience in which candidates assume full responsibility for a classroom under the supervision of a mentoring practitioner.

- Standard 4 requires that institutions design, implement, and evaluate curriculum and experiences that will help candidates work successfully with all students, including students from diverse racial and socioeconomic backgrounds, as well as with students with exceptionalities. The standard stresses the importance of behaviors that reflect fairness when working with P–12 students and the belief that all students can learn. It further expects that candidates have the opportunity to interact with diverse faculty members, diverse peers, and diverse P–12 students.

Standards 1 and 4 reveal a strong overlap with the emergent knowledge base. As demonstrated in Table 4.1, many of the elements in Standard 1 correspond to the types of knowledge, skills, and professional dispositions indicated in the emergent knowledge base. The purpose of Standard 1 is to ensure that institutions collect assessment data demonstrating that candidates have acquired the knowledge, skills, and professional dispositions needed to help all students learn.

The rubric for Standard 4, which provides a more detailed description of what the standard calls for, indicates that programs must ensure that candidates (1) understand the importance of diversity in teaching and learning; (2) learn to incorporate diversity in their lesson planning; (3) become aware of the different teaching and learning styles; and (4) are able to adapt instruction and service for all students, including students with exceptionalities. The standard goes on to expect that candidates have opportunities to have structured field experiences in school settings with diverse P–12 students.

NCATE is sometimes criticized from the left for being far too conservative in its expectations toward diversity and from the right for being too liberal in its expectations. In reality, NCATE has forged a middle ground that encourages institutions (1) to design and evaluate the curriculum related to diversity in the teaching and learning context; (2) to identify and assess proficiencies related to diversity in the teaching and learning context; (3) to provide candidates with experiences working with diverse students, including students with exceptionalities; and (4) to evaluate the institutional intention and attention given to the recruitment and retention of teacher candidates and faculty members from diverse ethnic/racial backgrounds.

Because the current set of standards was phased in over a five-year period (2000–2004), the full impact of the revised standards and revised accreditation system on teachers still in training may not

Table 4.1   A Comparison of the Knowledge Base for Teacher
Education and NCATE Standard 1: Candidate Knowledge,
Skills, and Dispositions

Knowledge Base: What teachers should know and be able to teach, as described in *A Good Teacher in Every Classroom* (Darling-Hammond & Snowden, 2005)	**NCATE Unit Standard 1:** Candidate Knowledge, Skills, and Dispositions (NCATE, 2002)
Know their subject well and know how to teach it to students	Candidates know the subject matter they plan to teach (content element). Teacher candidates have a broad knowledge of instructional strategies that draws upon content and pedagogical knowledge and skills (pedagogical content knowledge element).
Understand how children learn and develop	[Candidates] know the ways children and adolescents learn and develop and the relationship of these to learning (professional knowledge element).
Be able to observe, monitor, and assess children to gain accurate feedback about their learning and development	[Candidates] focus on student learning as shown in their assessment of student learning, use of assessment in instruction, and development of meaningful learning experiences (student learning element).
Know themselves—understand their own language and culture and know how to learn about other cultures with different language patterns and ways of knowing	[Candidates] understand language acquisition; cultural influences on learning; exceptionalities; diversity of student populations, families, and communities; and inclusion and equity in classrooms and schools (supporting explanation).
Be able to develop a curriculum and learning activities that connect what they know about their students to what the students need to learn	[Candidates] plan instruction based on knowledge of subject matter, students, families, the community, and curriculum goals.
Know how to teach specific subject matter in ways that are accessible, anticipating and addressing student conceptions and misconceptions	[Candidates] facilitate student learning of subject matter through presentations of the content in clear and meaningful ways (pedagogical content knowledge element).

(Continued)

Table 4.1   (Continued)

	Note: Institutions are also expected to meet standards developed by the specialized professional organizations that include a more detailed description of content and pedagogy in given fields of specialization.
Know how to develop and use assessments that measure learning standards and how to use the results to plan teaching that will address student learning needs	[Candidates] focus on student learning as shown in their assessment of student learning, use of assessment in instruction, and development of meaningful learning experiences.
Know how to use systematic inquiry, including how to observe an individual child in interaction with different tasks and other students to diagnose his or her needs	[Candidates] develop the knowledge base for analyzing student learning and practice by collecting data and assessing student learning through case studies and field and other experiences. They might examine student work samples for evidence of learning and develop lesson plans to help students who are having problems understanding the concepts being taught (supporting explanation).
Be able to evaluate why children may be responding or behaving in particular ways given the context of the classroom, the individual nature of the learning challenges, and the child's life outside school	[Candidates] consider the school, family, and community contexts in which they work and the prior experience of students to develop meaningful learning experiences (professional and pedagogical knowledge and skills element).
Be able to develop interventions, track changes, and revise their instructional strategies as necessary (pp. 27–28)	[Candidates] are able to create instructional opportunities adapted to diverse learners (supporting explanation).

yet be obvious. However, two interim reviews of institutions conducted by NCATE reveal that important changes are taking place. In 2004, as part of its regular review cycle, NCATE conducted a survey of over 1,000 deans and NCATE coordinators at accredited institutions and those in the accreditation pipeline (Mitchell & Yamagishi,

2004). The purpose of the survey was to determine the appropriateness and effectiveness of the unit standards from the perspectives of institutional representatives.[4]

Overall, 95% of the deans and NCATE coordinators who completed the survey indicated that their candidates benefit from attending an institution that has been accredited based on the NCATE Unit Standards. According to respondents, their programs are more cohesive and have stronger field experience components as a result of NCATE accreditation. A total of 84% of survey respondents agreed or strongly agreed that as a result of working with the NCATE Unit Standards, their faculty demonstrate more attention to candidate knowledge and skills related to helping all students learn. Significantly, 77% of respondents agreed or strongly agreed that their programs demonstrate a greater commitment to diversity as reflected in curriculum and field experiences, and 58% agreed or strongly agreed that as a result of working with the standards, the commitment to diversity resulted in increased numbers of teacher candidates and faculty members from diverse backgrounds. Comments indicated that some respondents felt that their institutions' commitment to diversity was strong already, and only reinforced by the NCATE standards. The survey revealed that NCATE accreditation can be a mechanism for change and continuous improvement, and an avenue for sharing important components of the emergent knowledge base with preservice teachers.

Overall, 95% of the deans and NCATE coordinators who completed the survey indicated that their candidates benefit from attending an institution that has been accredited based on the NCATE Unit Standards.

NCATE also conducted a study of institutional responses to its current standards and accreditation system based on a review of 58 Board of Examiner Reports written in fall 2003 by NCATE accreditation teams (Mitchell, Allen, & Ehrenberg, 2005). Because of NCATE's transition plan, the institutions were not yet expected to be fully implementing the standards, so the study was an "early look" at institutional responses. The study, like the survey, found that educator preparation programs are changing, in large part as a result of working with the NCATE standards. Faculty members within programs are collaborating more and thinking programmatically about course content and assessment. The programs are working more with P–12 practitioners to structure field experiences and to develop assessments that are aligned with standards. Finally, programs are making changes to existing courses, adding and deleting courses, and redesigning assessments based on an analysis of assessment data generated by their assessment systems. While these changes are positive, the study revealed that the nature of the work is evolutionary and continuous. Overall, the study, like the survey, highlights the potential of NCATE accreditation to provide structure for educator preparation programs as they, in turn, provide preservice and inservice teachers with the foundational knowledge and skills necessary to be effective teachers of all students.

CONCLUSION

The hallmark of a profession is the development of a body of knowledge that beginning practitioners must know and be able to put into practice. Educators are beginning to agree on a codified body of knowledge, skills, and professional dispositions. This emergent knowledge base is a prerequisite for effective educators who are able to help all students grow and develop intellectually, socially, and emotionally. Mastering this complex knowledge base—and fitting it together with the wisdom derived from practice—is the foundation of expertise in teaching.

The road to expertise is marked by formal knowledge and conceptual understanding. In order to help as many beginning teachers as possible travel this road, NCATE provides the structure for complex organizations like SCDEs to develop and implement curricula and assessments based on the emergent knowledge base.

All of the problems in urban schools cannot be solved by teacher education. However, in helping institutions to prepare effective educators, the profession, through its accrediting body, is taking a huge step in the right direction. While the research has not yet been produced that definitively links all of the various aspects of teacher education curricula to effective teaching (Zeichner & Conklin, 2005), the wisdom of practice and scientific research from multiple fields point to an emergent knowledge base that is important for teachers to understand and draw upon, if they are to work successfully with all students, and particularly with students from culturally and socioeconomically diverse backgrounds.

REFERENCES

Berliner, D. C. (2005, August). Our impoverished view of educational reform. *Teachers College Record.* Retrieved 12/28/05 from http://www.tcrecord.org

Bransford, J. D., Brown, A. L., & Cockling, R. R. (1999). *How people learn: Brain, mind, experience, and school.* Washington, DC: National Academies Press.

Cochran-Smith, M. (2003). Teacher education's Bermuda Triangle: Dichotomy, mythology, and amnesia. *Journal of Teacher Education, 54,* 275–279.

Cochran-Smith, M., & Fries, K. (2005). Researching teacher education in changing times: Politics and Paradigms. In M. Cochran-Smith & K. Zeichner (Eds.), *Studying teacher education: The report of the AERA Panel on Research and Teacher Education* (pp. 69–110). Mahwah, NJ: Lawrence Erlbaum.

Comer, J. (1980). *School power: Implications of an intervention project.* New York: The Free Press.

Cuban, L., & Usdan, M. (Eds.). (2003). *Powerful reforms with shallow roots: Improving America's urban schools.* New York: Teacher's College Press.

Darling-Hammond, L., & Bransford, J. (Eds.). (2005). *Preparing teachers for a changing world: What teachers should learn and be able to do.* San Francisco: Jossey-Bass.

Darling-Hammond, L., & Snowden, J. (Eds.). (2005). *A good teacher in every classroom: Preparing the highly qualified teachers our children deserve.* San Francisco: Jossey-Bass.

Donavan, M. S., Bransford, J. D., & Pelligrino, J. W. (1999). *How people learn: Bridging research and practice.* Washington, DC: National Academy Press.

Epstein, J. L., Sanders, M. G., Simon, B. S., Salinas, K. C., Jansorn, N. R., & Van Voortus, F. L. (2002). *School, family, and community partnerships: Your handbook for action* (2nd ed.). Thousand Oaks, CA: Corwin Press.

Fetler, M. (1999, March 26). High school staff characteristics and mathematics test results. *Education Policy Analysis Archives, 7*(9). Retrieved December 12, 2005, from http://epaa.asu.edu/epaa/v7n9.html

Friedman, T. L. (2005). *The world is flat: A brief history of the twenty-first century.* New York: Farrar, Straus and Giroux.

Gladwell, M. (2005). *Blink.* New York: Little, Brown.

Hollins, E., & Guzman, M. T. (2005). Research on preparing teachers for diverse populations. In M. Cochran-Smith & K. Zeichner (Eds.), *Studying teacher education: The report of the AERA Panel on Research and Teacher Education* (pp. 477–548). Mahwah, NJ: Lawrence Erlbaum.

Irvine, J. J. (2003). *Educating teachers for diversity: Seeing with a cultural eye.* New York: Teachers College Press.

Kozol, J. (1991). *Savage inequalities.* New York: Crown.

Kozol, J. (1995). *Amazing grace.* New York: Crown.

Ladson-Billings, G. (1994). *The dreamkeepers: Successful teachers of African American children.* San Francisco: Jossey-Bass.

Mitchell, A. S. (1996). The work lives of urban teachers: 1960–1990 (Doctoral dissertation, University of California, Berkeley, 1996). *UMI Dissertation Services, 9723117.*

Mitchell, A. S. (2000). African American teachers: The roles they play. In M. Sanders (Ed.), *Schooling students placed at risk: Research, policy, and practice in the education of poor and minority adolescents* (pp. 163–185). Mahwah, NJ: Lawrence Erlbaum.

Mitchell, A., Allen, S., & Ehrenberg, P. (2005). Spotlight on schools of education: How 58 institutions responded to NCATE standards 1 and 2. Washington, DC: National Council for Accreditation of Teacher Education.

Mitchell, A. S., & Yamagishi, Y. (2004). The results are in: What deans and NCATE coordinators think about the NCATE Unit Standards. Washington, DC: National Council for Accreditation of Teacher Education.

National Commission on Teaching and America's Future. (1996). *What matters most: Teaching for America's future.* New York: Author.

National Commission on Teaching and America's Future. (2004). *Fifty years after Brown v. Board of Education: A two-tiered education system.* Washington, DC: Author.

National Council for Accreditation of Teacher Education. (2002). *Professional standards for the accreditation of schools, colleges, and departments of education, 2002 edition.* Washington, DC: Author.

Nieto, S. (2003). *What keeps teachers going?* New York: Columbia College Press.

Noddings, N. (1992). *The challenge to care in schools: An alternative approach to education.* New York: Teachers College Press.

Reich, R. B. (1992). The *work of nations: Preparing ourselves for 21st century Capitalism.* New York: Vintage Books.

Tyack, D. (1990). Restructuring in historical perspective: Tinkering toward utopia. *Teachers College Record, 92,* 170–191.

Villegas, A. M., & Lucas, T. (2002). *Educating culturally responsive teachers: A coherent approach.* Albany, NY: SUNY Press.

Wenglinsky, H. (2002, February 13). How schools matter: The link between teacher classroom practices and student academic performance.

Education Policy Analysis Archives, *10*(12). Retrieved December 12, 2005, from http://epaa.asu.edu/epaa/v10n12

Zeichner, K., & Conklin, H. (2005). Teacher education programs. In M. Cochran-Smith & K. Zeichner (Eds.), *Studying teacher education: The report of the AERA Panel on Research and Teacher Education* (pp. 645–736). Mahwah, NJ: Lawrence Erlbaum.

NOTES

1. The opinions expressed in this chapter are the author's and do not reflect the policies or beliefs of any of the organizations mentioned.

2. Constituent members include founding members such as the American Association of Colleges for Teacher Education (AACTE) and the National Education Association (NEA). Other constituent organizations include the Council of Chief State School Officers, the American Federation of Teachers, the National Association of State Boards of Education, the Association of Teacher Educators, the National Association of Teachers of Mathematics, and similar organizations of teachers, policy makers, and specialized practitioners.

3. The remaining standards are Standards 5 and 6. Standard 5 is on faculty qualifications, performance, and development. Standard 6 is on governance and resources.

4. After conducting follow-up activities, the response rate for the survey was 66%. All respondents, however, did not answer all of the questions posed. Of the respondents, 34% identified themselves as deans, 52% identified themselves as NCATE coordinators, and 14% identified themselves as serving in both roles.

CHAPTER FIVE

CAPTURE, INSPIRE, TEACH!

Reflections on High Expectations for Every Learner

STEPHEN PETERS

M y passion is to teach. My calling and purpose in life is to teach. Many of you who are reading this article can relate to this because you, too, have been called to teach in some form. In a time when our children need us the most—living in a world with such uncertainty, lost with little hope of realizing their own dreams and aspirations—who can they depend on to create the change needed to provide a better world for them? Our teachers, support staff, and administrators surely are making a serious attempt to provide hope and service, but it has become increasingly difficult to feel confident that our children's futures look bright. Homes and schools are so different today, making it more difficult to make the connection necessary to truly educate today's young people. While athletes and movie stars live the life our children dream about, the majority of our children and teachers have reached a "disconnect" to the degree that it concerns most of us who understand our calling.

According to a recent article in *USA Today* (Reeve, 2005), laws such as the No Child Left Behind Act (NCLB) of 2001 are "failing the test on minority students." Now NCLB is entering its fourth year of promoting education reform through testing and accountability. For large-city school districts—especially those with high numbers of students who are poor, Latino, black, or English language learners—the odds of failing to meet the act's high-proficiency hurdles this year are good. Why? Because the rules are stacked against the very low-achieving schools they are supposed to help.

Moreover, the act aims to close the achievement gap between white and minority students in reading and math, but the law puts schools serving the neediest students at greater disadvantage. Schools in smaller districts and with a majority of white students have lower and fewer hurdles to meet proficiency goals. One size does not fit all.

A research and policy think tank at Harvard University looked at districts that needed improvement in the 2004–2005 school year (U.S. Department of Education, 2005). Researchers focused on Illinois, Georgia, Virginia, California, New York, and Arizona. They found that districts that had failed to make the "adequate yearly progress" required by the law had high numbers of students who were black, Latino, low-income, and/or English language learners. In Illinois, for example, districts needing improvement were nearly 30% black, nearly 25% Latino, and more than 52% low-income.

Proficiency targets/goals set an unrealistic hurdle for these students, who enter school with lower skills and are required to make faster progress. This is like putting a slow runner 50 yards behind at the start of a race and expecting him or her to finish with the fastest.

Proponents of the act would say this indicates that the law works by identifying those who need the most help, but those of us who are on the front line have always been aware of who is most in need. Moreover, when the accountability rules are flawed and don't accurately measure progress or account for diversity, one would have to begin to question the act's overall effectiveness or whether it truly serves the best interests of all children.

A better approach, as offered by the Civil Rights Project (National Black Caucus of State Legislators, 2001), would include setting more realistic performance goals and giving schools more time to improve student performance.

Understanding the need to make remarkable improvement in the core subject areas like math and reading, we must tap children's other interests in order to get to the core elements of learning. I believe that unconditional positive regard is a must for our children's mental health.

I believe that unconditional positive regard is a must for our children's mental health.

We must rise to the occasion as never before to deliver quality to *all* of our children—the same quality we want delivered to our own biological children. America's children deserve nothing less.

In all of my travels and work with schools, teachers, support staff, administrators, parents, and communities, there is little evidence that would lead me to believe that an overwhelming number of children sitting in classrooms in America have no desire to learn. I am convinced that we live in a time when it has become imperative we find ways to ensure success for every child we encounter daily.

As a teacher, my passion was working with children who at many junctures in their lives had been *eliminated*—eliminated from conversations, dreams, hope, and learning. My experiences with children from low-socioeconomic and disadvantaged backgrounds laid the foundation for how I proceeded to accept others who would come to depend on me to teach them. Children today are clearly different from when I grew up many years ago. In those days, school and education synonymously were at the very center of our lives. Families created the spectrum of our underlying and exposed belief systems that carried us through our day with a clear picture of who we were, where we came from, and where we belonged.

Expectations were high, and we felt the responsibility of representing our families. Therefore, anything that happened to us also happened to our families. I was told many years ago that "no one rises to low expectations." As I matriculated through public school, I always carried this thought with me. There were times when I wanted to give up, thinking I was in over my head. One of the determining factors for me through those difficult times was the fact that I knew I had a support system in place, ready to intervene on a moment's notice. Times have truly changed.

The groundwork for this chapter was laid after a speech I gave last year in Cincinnati, Ohio, to a group of high school student leaders. Many of my talks to groups of students had left me feeling a need to dig deeper, express myself more openly, encourage and challenge as well as give tough love to many who struggled with aspects of life I knew little about. As educators, we have a responsibility to every student we teach or encounter to at least have general knowledge of his or her culture, learning styles, surroundings, and likes or dislikes.

DREAMS AND ASPIRATIONS

My audience that day was extremely bright and diverse. It included a deaf student who was very much involved in our training and discussion with the help of her fellow students and the ability of adults who made the connection. My major theme was "discovering your place and purpose in this world."

During the course of my speech, I placed a photo of a famous rap music star on the screen and asked who he was. They immediately responded correctly to this question as well as to many that followed pertaining to him. They knew all of his songs and their lyrics, where he grew up, where he lived now, where his next concert was going to be, whom he dated, and on and on.

I was not surprised by this, nor was I surprised about what was to follow. I offered a hundred-dollar bill to any student present who could answer my next question: "Who is the current U.S. Secretary of Education?" Not one student could answer correctly—a teachable moment for me!

Students today place their attention and focus on issues and subjects that are relevant to them. Knowledge about the rap star was imbedded in both their minds and spirits that day because they spend an enormous amount of time watching music videos and reading gossip columns and magazines that feed them the information they so desire about their favorite entertainers and artists. My question about the entertainer interested them. My second question did not— there was no knowledge base or foundation for any of them to draw from. The base for the first question was MTV, VH1, BET, *Source* magazine, and many more.

My teachable moment went like this: "Students, it is impressive that you all have such expert knowledge about a subject. It is even more impressive that you have such passion to go along with that knowledge. But knowing who this rap star is and what the titles and lyrics of his songs are is not relevant in your life at this juncture. As you attempt to graduate from high school and, for some of you, matriculate into college and graduate school, please understand this simple fact: My first question will not appear on your SAT or ACT. My second question might."

Their eyes wandered for a moment, and a few hands went into the air. The first student responded, "How long does that hundred-dollar deal last?" We smiled, but we all left that day with a feeling of concern.

A few days later, I received an e-mail from one of the students who was in my audience that day. She identified herself and went on to share that I had made some critical points that day; she told me that she had gone home and done some research on the question I posed. She went on to say, "Mr. Peters, you are so right. We do concentrate on things that are not important to our futures. Everything seems so shallow, temporary, and meaningless." She did her homework and shared the fact that she now knows who holds the post of U.S. Secretary of Education.

My experiences with young people always prompt questions in my mind about how we might be able to *capture* them better and hold onto them until they understand the simple facts in life. Then, we can help them discover their natural gifts, and devise a plan for them to develop these gifts and a vehicle for them to use them in and for the world. Isn't this what education is all about?

Mrs. Grant would look us in the eye and say, "You all are ready for the next level. Do you know why you are so ready? Because I taught you!"

In my travels, I have had the unique pleasure of seeing what I have come to call "real teaching," the kind of teaching Mrs. Grant did when I was in her English class. At the end of the year, she would look us in the eye and say, "You all are ready for the next level. Do you know why you are so ready? Because I taught you!" There was such pride in the delivery of her service to her students. Another teacher, Mr. Pendergrass, would come to school each day dressed as if he were the CEO of a Fortune 500 company. These experiences made a huge impact on the person I would become.

Currently, at the end of the school year, our students are not hearing what Mrs. Grant would tell us; they are hearing something totally different. They are hearing, "Students, we have come to the close of another school year. I don't know where each of you will go, but you are going away from here!"

Unfortunately, many are going to the next grade or level unprepared to function. This results in one of our country's fastest-growing trends: high school dropouts. Current research tells us that there are more African American males going to prison than to college. According to a recent *Newsweek* article (Cossel, 2005), "It's no longer just a case of boys will be boys." Thirty years ago, the percentage of male undergraduates on college campuses was 58%. At present, the percentage is 44%. At every juncture of schooling in America, male students are losing ground. From absent fathers to distracting toys to teaching that ignores how boys develop and learn, we have to trace the causes and understand that we are dealing not only with a new generation of children, we are also dealing with a new generation of educators.

As educators, we have become accustomed to using the latest buzzwords or politically correct terminology that matches the latest reform efforts or legislature. A simple approach is needed to get us back to the basics of understanding what it is to learn and why it is important that we all learn together and for a lifetime.

As I stood in the hallway of my first school as principal, I could literally *feel* the need for the culture of that school to change immediately. Culture can be defined as a way of life, especially as it relates to socially transmitted habits, traditions, customs, and beliefs that characterize a particular group of people. It also includes the actions, behaviors, practices, attitudes, norms and values, and communication (language) patterns and traits. Culture is the lens through which we see the world. It is the context within which we operate and make sense of what we see. It influences how we process learning, solve problems, and teach.

Many of our teachers realized at that time that we were facing a crisis. We all realized that we needed to rally around each other to make something happen or many more of our children were going to be lost to this "new" world that was developing. We made significant progress in a short period of time through a concerted effort. We believed that having high expectations would result in our concentrating on successes versus failures. In the public schools of America today, it's not that our students are not reaching our expectations. The fact of the matter is they *are* reaching them. The expectations are simply too low.

Classrooms today do not look the same as they did a decade ago. Major demographic shifts have occurred and led to increasing numbers of culturally, linguistically, and socioeconomically diverse students in our schools. At the same time, NCLB and the resulting requirement that schools report disaggregated data have focused a spotlight on the achievement gaps that have persisted for years between children of color, children in poverty, and English language learning (ELL) students and their mainstream peers.

While recent reports indicate that some progress is being made to close these gaps, significant inequities continue to exist for a wide range of educational indicators including grades, scores on standardized tests, dropout rates, and participation in higher education.

Currently, as I work with schools and school divisions, I have become increasingly passionate about the need for educators to understand the power and authority we have to restore hope to our students—or to destroy it. Many districts are searching for techniques and people to help make a greater difference in our schools every day. Our children require much more. A conscious, reflective change strategy is urgently needed for our schools.

When I began in education more than 20 years ago, we were at a critical juncture of change. The dynamics of the family were beginning to break down, resulting in a different student reporting to school and the classroom each day. We were dealing with a more distracted, withdrawn, frustrated student. We were also dealing with a different and more frustrated teacher. I truly believe because of

It is important to understand the only way to effectively teach a student of today's world. We must first capture *that student.*

these changing dynamics, homes are not what they used to be, schools are not what they used to be, teachers are not what we used to be, and certainly students are not what they used to be.

It is important to understand the only way to effectively teach a student of today's world. We must first *capture* that student. To capture means to seize, to take or secure. I was captured by many of my teachers while a youngster in school. I was amazed by their presence and passion. They seemed to feel that because we were being taught by them, it was impossible for us to fail at anything. They graced our lives.

Mark Anthony Garret recalls growing up in foster care throughout his life. Moving from home to home, school to school, he wonders how he came to be who he is today. Mark was placed into foster care two hours after he was born. Today, Mark is a national and international radio talk show host and motivational speaker. He credits his success to a teacher—not just any teacher, but a phenomenal teacher, one who would not give up on him, one who understood the dreams and aspirations of this young African American student.

"She truly believed in me," he recalls, "and not for a moment did she doubt that I would make it in the world regardless of my circumstances. She always stated, it's not where you come from, but it's all about where you are going."

Teachers like those in Mark's life understood their ability to change children's lives. They understood the process of capturing and inspiring. Long ago, there was enormous pride in the teaching profession; today, for many reasons, our profession has suffered great losses. The major loss has been the simple pride of being a teacher. We need to regain that pride quickly as we attempt to bring our best stuff each day to a generation that desperately needs our best.

A CONSCIOUS, REFLECTIVE STRATEGY

Understanding today's youth is a beginning for many of us who work with young people on a daily basis. Years ago, the framework of the family provided both the structure and the stability children needed to go out into the world ready to learn. Major encumbrances were not there to impede the progress of the young mind embracing new knowledge and experiences that would shape the person he or she would soon become.

As we trace the decades of our past, themes begin to develop about the foundation that families once provided for their children. I grew up the youngest of six children and now know that my parents must have had a difficult time continuously putting food on the table. I didn't know this as a child because I *was* a child. Today, children as young as four are aware of the daily pressures battering their families.

I do believe there is hope as we begin to prepare a generation for bright futures. Schools and those working in them have to be more than adequately prepared to deliver quality services to today's students. Let's now examine four basic principles that will help prepare and sustain our efforts.

EXAMINING YOUR KNOWLEDGE AND BELIEFS

It is important that we become conscious of our own beliefs, feelings, and experiences related to the differences we experience on a day-to-day basis. This will help us separate our own prejudices from the immediate circumstances, thus facilitating a more fair and just outcome for all students. What we believe has a profound and powerful effect on how we behave; therefore, it is important that we understand and process what we believe.

I was told once that belief is confidence in an alleged fact without positive proof. It is easy to see how one who believes this might get into trouble by simply acting on that belief. Every person has a belief system, and the strength of our beliefs about any particular idea depends on how central they are to our belief system. Rokeach (1973) defines beliefs this way: "[Belief] . . . transcends attitudes towards objects and situations, ideology, presentations of self to others, evaluations, judgments, justifications, comparisons of self with others and attempts to influence others."

Rokeach's research has revealed that the more strongly one holds a belief, the more resistant it is to change. This implies that we weight the strength of our beliefs about different things and situations. Personally, this is a signal to me to make an effort to fully understand how I came to feel so strongly about what I believe.

Ask yourself what you believe about a certain group of people who are different from yourself. How strong are your beliefs about this group? Now think about the human diversity in your classroom or school. What beliefs do you have about children of different racial groups? About those with different physical capabilities? More important, what do you feel about their capacity to learn?

Understanding students—their histories, cultures, and way of life—will enable you to teach them more effectively.

When examining your beliefs, it is important to feel at ease to share and ask any type of question, so learning about each other can occur. A safe environment is essential. Understanding, for example, your personal histories and experiences with people of other races or socioeconomic status makes you conscious of the different responses you have to people of different races and status. Remaining ignorant about obvious societal problems such as racism or discrimination against people with disabilities denies the reality of human life and existence, but particularly denies the right of every student regardless of race, socioeconomic status, or class to learn and receive an education that would set them on a path of success thereafter.

Understanding students—their histories, cultures, and way of life—will enable you to teach them more effectively. As I laid the groundwork for my book, *Do You Know Enough About Me to Teach Me?*, many of my concerns about how all students were treated came into play. Students I interviewed were honest and candid about how they were treated, and some of the things I heard were not good. Not good at all.

Your beliefs affect how you treat students, just as your beliefs, knowledge, and understanding of those in your own cultural group influence how you feel about them and how you treat them. Not knowing the history and culture of all the students you face puts you at a disadvantage. You (and, even more, your students) are robbed of rich histories, interactions, and opportunities to learn from each other. Ask yourself, *do you know enough about them to teach them?*

PROFESSIONAL BEHAVIOR AND INSTRUCTIONAL DELIVERY

My reflections on professional behavior are quite simple. All of us need to become more accountable to ourselves as well as to others, and we can only benefit from conscious thinking and rethinking of what we say and do. As a teacher of teachers, I have learned the true value of giving myself feedback and asking for it from others.

There was a time when teachers were very aware of how they dressed for school and the impact their appearance would have on their students that day. My ninth-grade teacher always came to school with a shirt and tie each day. He believed that was the proper thing to do. It sent a message to us students that he thought highly of us and of his profession. He was not only reflective about his appearance, but also about his teaching and delivery of information to us. I am convinced that his reflective questions helped him become the great teacher he presented to us each day.

Becoming more reflective will assist you in becoming more conscientious about your work. Purposeful reflection affords us an opportunity to discern the root of behavioral issues that arise with others, whether it occurs with coworkers, parents, or students. I often find reflection to be the very foundation of renewing my purpose. Effective teachers and school leaders understand their purpose.

Instructional reflection always helped me understand the human elements of all of my students. When I was a classroom teacher,

I attempted to gather as much information as possible about my students so I would be in a position to offer quality services to each of them. I kept a journal of things that occurred throughout the day, examining my role in each scenario. Personal reflection about relationships and delivery of instruction was critical to having my students feel a part of a whole versus a fragmented piece of our class structure, as they felt so often in the world.

As educators, we truly face our share of obstacles. Reflecting on our part in every situation will lay the framework for developing meaningful relationships with our students. They will appreciate every effort we make in understanding our role in their daily lives.

UNDERSTANDING THE CHANGE PROCESS

Becoming aware and conscious of my own beliefs, experiences, and responses to change was critical to responding effectively to the needs of the diverse population of students, teachers, and staff members. I also determined that the more I understood about the ways in which change occurred, the more I could anticipate the journey, which enabled me to better manage my responses to it. Becoming sensitive to what is happening in the world around us and how events affect us personally and at school is very important in understanding our responses to change.

Research on successful school reform or major change in schools reveals that it requires several years—usually a minimum of three—to bring about change. It further reveals that teachers and their instructional practices should be at the core of change (Fullan & Hargreaves, 1992; Goodlad, 1990). Historically, teachers have been on the periphery of change and are seen in very traditional ways as having command of their isolated classrooms, but not as leaders in schools.

I recall my first year in a school that was first in things you would want to be last in and last in things you would want to be first in. Change was not a bad word to us; we embraced change because we wanted things to be better. We wanted our environment to be better, adult and student attitudes and behavior to be better, attendance to be better, and student achievement to be better. Moreover, we wanted the community's perception of us to be better. The desire for change was certainly present for us, but we needed more.

Today, I engage teachers, support staff, and administrators in my inservice training sessions in discussions about why people change. It's always an interesting exchange of information, knowledge, wisdom, and experiences. I share that there are four typical reasons people change and then ask which of these four reasons has the longest-lasting effect? The four reasons are

1. Desire

2. Pressure/Heat

3. Rewards/Incentives

4. Environment

Which of these four reasons would *you* choose as having the longest-lasting effect on change? Let's examine this further. If we choose desire, the change that occurs only lasts as long as I have the desire to change. If we choose pressure/heat, the change that occurs only last as long as the person, place, or thing exerting the pressure or heat is present. If we choose rewards/incentives, change will only last as long as the rewards or incentives last. If we choose environment, we are correct, because when we change an environment, we are able to sustain change.

As leader, my responsibility was to make sure the adults in our building felt needed; validated; affirmed; and, more important, appreciated.

In our school, where we were overwhelmed with obstacles every day, we chose to change our environment. There were those who found it difficult to change because, according to them, "We have been doing this a lot longer than most." Inevitably, they would come to find that quantity does not necessarily yield quality. We decided that synergy would be our vehicle to achieving better results than we were getting. As leader, my responsibility was to make sure the adults in our building felt needed; validated; affirmed; and, more important, appreciated. We began going about our business in a different way. As Stephen Covey states, we began with the end in mind.

This process would prove difficult to say the least, but the results we began getting after a short time indicated that we were definitely on the right track. Our faculty and staff attendance was our first indicator that things were improving. Student attendance followed, with the drop in office referrals coming as our favorite surprise. That meant teachers were beginning to be able to do what they came to school to do: teach.

If someone were to ask me (and many did) what two factors contributed to effective change in our building, I would have to reply passion and purpose. Our staff truly began to revisit why they became teachers and to understand the power and authority they had each day to build a child up or to destroy a child. When our students began to feel the intensity of care and concern from the adults in our school each day, they could not do anything else but choose to respond.

The change described above may not happen in your school this way, or it may take longer to have those indicators line up the way you want them to. The bottom line is that when you change an environment, you construct the framework for good things to happen for children. In the process, schools begin to serve their intended purpose: to educate our children and prepare them to take their rightful places in the world.

DISCOVERING OUR NEEDED RESOURCES

The next lens of the Capture, Inspire, Teach! model focuses on building relationships with individuals and groups who have a stake in providing effective educational experiences for all of our children. This network begins with families and then spreads to larger institutions and organizations in our respective communities.

The influence of the home on children's success at school is critical in so many ways. Public schools and communities are now feeling the effects of the breakdown of the home on many different fronts. Our children are coming to school with little or no focus, desire, or connection to their teachers.

Unless we totally commit ourselves to increasing the involvement and participation of the family as we find it in our school communities, we will continue to dance alone. Parents and guardians of school-aged children in America truly do want good things for their children. But we must remember that many of these parents or family members did not have pleasant experiences themselves as children in our schools. As I visited and observed one of my schools in an inner-city setting, I couldn't help but notice the signs in the main parking area and on the front doors to the school. The signs reminded anyone coming to visit that if they parked in the wrong space, their car would be towed. Another sign read in bold letters, "Trespassers will be prosecuted."

If one were confused about what trespassing is, he or she would be more inclined to stay away just to be safe. We have to be careful what messages we send to our families and community members. There are hidden resources around all of our schools. We simply need to begin to take a different approach to tapping into them and providing a place in which everyone feels a part of the process of change. *We* have to change.

RAPID RESULTS

I am often asked how one might experience immediate results when attempting to turn a school around for the better. My response is to say, begin with the self. That is always a great starting point. It is extremely difficult for us to change others, but more manageable to change ourselves. Listed below are a few other suggestions:

- Know yourself and how you respond to challenges.
- Be aware of human differences in your student population. Examine your attitudes toward them.
- Identify your own learning style, as well as your students' learning styles.
- Teach critical thinking in the context of awareness.
- Teach self-control, self-respect, and respect of others.
- Foster a positive school climate and culture.
- Create win-win situations as often as possible.
- Allow students to experience real stability and consistency.
- Realize your own *power* as it relates to making a difference in your student's lives.
- Involve the school community in school activities as much as possible.
- Always ask the question, "Is it in the best interest of all students?"
- Remember always,
  HIGH EXPECTATIONS = CONCENTRATION = MANIFESTATION.

Enormous challenges must be overcome to create greater opportunities for all students to achieve success in school. The primary challenge is developing and implementing a comprehensive agenda for reform. We cannot continue to expect students to meet with success if they are sitting in classrooms with 30-plus students, all learning at a different pace and in different ways. Neither can we expect our profession to remain one that commands enduring respect if we fail to bring our best stuff to school every single day. Today's students require that we bring everything we have to give, one day at a time. They are hungry for success, and they desire a better way of life. We must find a constructive, realistic way of delivering the deliverables.

It is extremely difficult for us to change others, but more manageable to change ourselves.

My teacher thought I was smarter than I was—so I was. It's amazing how we rise to meet the expectations of others when they are realistic, clear, and relevant. Learning for me in this teacher's classroom was fun, invigorating, and meaningful. She truly captured all of us in an instant and had us in line the very first day of school. This teacher did not need to send kids to the principal's office as punishment; she enlisted us as part of her management team. We need more students becoming members of school management teams. It gives them purpose.

Many great things come in threes. Here are three trios for you to consider:

Passion, Purpose, and Persistence

Passion brings intensity to any situation, while purpose reminds us of why we do what we do. Persistence keeps us on our track of realizing that failure truly is not an option for any of our students. They can't afford to fail, and we can't afford to let them.

Relationships, Rigor, and Relevance

Relationships are the key to any success you might have in your school or organization. Spend time understanding and cultivating healthy relationships, and your school will benefit greatly from your efforts. Rigor is defined and understood in several different ways. We must take time to examine our definition. It is important for us to comprehend the importance of what rigor is for each child we are responsible for educating. Relevance is at the heart of American society and truly impacts all ages, races, cultures, and organizations. We all concentrate on those things that have meaning for us. Our children should be at the top of that list.

Capture, Inspire, Teach!

To capture means to secure, seize, or take over. If students were being captured each day in classrooms all across America, what kind of future society would we have? Covey talks about "beginning with the end in mind." We need to begin visualizing success for all of the children we come into contact with each day. More important, as we go to sleep each night, we must ask ourselves, "Did I deliver quality services to all of my students today, the same quality I would want delivered to my own children at home?" We should all be answering that question with an unequivocal YES!

To inspire means to stimulate, arouse, or motivate. The question I ask teachers and others who work with children is this: How can you inspire if you are so uninspired?

We cannot expect children to become excited about learning if we are not excited about teaching and learning. That is a simple fact. Let's change the way we interact with our students. Let's excite them. Let's inspire them beyond their imaginations.

To teach means to provide with knowledge or help. According to this definition, today's youth are being taught. They are being provided with knowledge, they are being shown, but they are not being helped. The number-one influence on youth today is television and multimedia, with peer influence running a close second. Schools, churches, and homes are further down on that list for the second decade in a row.

I believe without a shadow of a doubt that we will see these children again later in our lives, the same children who are sitting in our classrooms today. Wouldn't it be something if one of them became your surgeon or your accountant or your grandchild's teacher? Or better yet, our president?

We have what it takes to make an enormous difference in our respective schools and school districts. Synergy is at the heart of the cause and requires us to understand that the efforts of more than one far outweigh the efforts of one. I am a teacher—ready, willing, and able to go the distance for a great cause, the great cause of education. Where would we be today without it?

I personally challenge each and every one of you to renew your energy, your passion and purpose. Teaching is not a job, it is a calling. We were called to teach. We should be proud to be a part of a profession that is so great. Let's represent our profession in such a manner that our students and the world see us for who we really are, the magicians who work magic in their lives and send them on their way to use their natural gifts and talents and walk in their purpose.

REFERENCES

Cossel, E. (2005, January 13). *Newsweek.*

Fullan, M., & Hargreaves, A. (1992). *Teacher development and educational change.* London: Falmer.

Goodlad, J. (1990). Teachers for our nation's schools. San Francisco: Jossey-Bass.

National Black Caucus of State Legislators. (2001, November). *Closing the achievement gap: Improving educational outcomes for African American children.* Washington, DC: Author. Available: http://www.nbcsl.com/news/pdf/cag.pdf

Peters, S. (2004). *Do you know enough about me to teach me?* Orangeburg, SC: Cecil Williams.

Reeve, J. (2005, October 26). Focus on test-taking leaves other skills behind. *USA Today,* p. 11A.

Rokeach, M. (1973). *The nature of human values.* New York: Free Press.

U.S. Department of Education. (2005). *Key reform strategies: An overview of research findings.* Washington, DC: Government Printing Office.

CHAPTER SIX

ALL OUR CHILDREN LEARNING

New Views on the Work of Benjamin S. Bloom

THOMAS R. GUSKEY

N ot all groups of students learn equally well in school. Some learn excellently, reach high levels of achievement, and reap the many positive benefits of that success. But many others learn less well and gain few of those positive benefits.

These gaps in the achievement of different groups of students have been evident for decades. In the 1960s, President Lyndon Johnson's "War on Poverty" focused directly on inequalities in the educational achievement of economically disadvantaged students and their more advantaged counterparts. The Economic Opportunity Act (EOA) of 1964, which established the Head

The gaps in the achievement of different groups of students have been evident for decades.

Start program, and the Elementary and Secondary Education Act (ESEA) of 1965, which created the Title I and Follow Through programs, were specific attempts to address these gaps in educational attainment.

In recent years, achievement gaps among different groups of students have attracted renewed scrutiny. Recognizing that a highly skilled workforce is essential for success in today's global economy, public officials have enacted new legislation that requires schools to focus on high levels of achievement for *all* students. These new laws compel school leaders to report student achievement results separately for various poverty, ethnicity, language, and disability subgroups. Not only must these leaders identify any achievement gaps among these different subgroups, they also must take specific steps to close them.

Over the years, educational researchers have studied these educational disparities extensively and have learned a great deal about reducing them. Unfortunately, many of those proposing new programs and strategies to close achievement gaps seem unaware of this important knowledge base. As a result, they simply "rediscover" well-established principles and end up making little real progress. To succeed in our efforts to close achievement gaps and to reach our goal of helping *all* students learn well, we must recognize this hard-earned knowledge base and then find ways to extend and enhance it in the context of today's classrooms and schools.

This chapter describes the work of one of the foremost contributors to that knowledge base: Benjamin S. Bloom. We will consider how Bloom conceptualized and addressed the problem of achievement gaps, as well as the success that he and his students achieved in resolving the problem through the use of mastery learning. We then will describe the essential elements of mastery learning, discuss common misinterpretations, and conclude with a summary of the research on its effects in various school contexts.

THE CONTRIBUTION OF BENJAMIN S. BLOOM

When researchers study a problem, they first try to reduce it to its simplest and most basic form. Educational researchers who study student achievement, for example, tend to view achievement gaps simply as a matter of "variation": students vary in their levels of achievement. Some students learn very well in school and achieve at high levels, while others learn less well and attain only modest levels. Whenever the achievement of two or more students is measured, this "variation" is evident.

The purpose of most research studies is to "explain" variation. Researchers make educated guesses, called hypotheses, about what factors contribute to identified differences among individuals or groups. They then manipulate those factors in carefully planned investigations to determine the effects. When they find a relationship between the factors that they manipulate and differences in the outcomes, they succeed in explaining variation.

One of the early researchers concerned with explaining variation in student achievement was Benjamin S. Bloom (see Guskey, 2006). In the early 1960s, Bloom's studies focused on individual differences in children, especially when it came to school learning. He recognized that many factors outside of school affect how well children learn, but also believed that educators have potentially strong influence as well (Bloom, 1964).

Bloom quickly discovered that there was relatively little variation in most teachers' instructional practices.

To determine the cause of these differences, Bloom began by observing teachers in their classrooms. He quickly discovered that there was relatively little variation in most teachers' instructional practices. The majority taught all of their students in much the same way and provided all with the same amount of time to learn. Students for whom these instructional methods and time were ideal learned excellently. However, the largest number of students found these methods and the amount of time to be only moderately appropriate and learned less well. Students for whom the instruction and time were inappropriate due to differences in their backgrounds or learning styles tended to learn very little. In other words, little variation in the teaching resulted in great variation in student learning outcomes. Under these conditions, the pattern of student achievement was similar to the normal curve distribution shown in Figure 6.1.

To attain better results and *reduce* this variation in student achievement, Bloom reasoned that we would have to *increase* variation in the teaching. That is, because students varied in their learning styles and aptitudes, we must diversify and differentiate instruction to better meet their individual learning needs. The challenge was to find practical ways to do this within the constraints of group-based classrooms so that *all* students learn well.

In searching for such a strategy, Bloom drew primarily from two sources of evidence. First, he considered the ideal teaching and

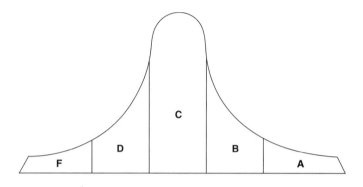

Figure 6.1   Distribution of Achievement in Traditional Classrooms

learning situation in which an excellent tutor is paired with each student. He was particularly influenced by the work of early pioneers in individualized instruction, especially Washburne (1922) and his Winnetka Plan, and Morrison (1926) and his University of Chicago Laboratory School experiments. In examining this evidence, Bloom tried to determine what critical elements in one-to-one tutoring and individualized instruction could be transferred to group-based classroom settings.

Second, Bloom looked at studies of the learning strategies of academically successful students, especially the work of Dollard and Miller (1950). From this research, he tried to identify the activities of high-achieving students in group-based classrooms that distinguish them from their less successful classmates.

Bloom believed it was reasonable for teachers to organize the concepts and skills they wanted students to learn into instructional units. He also considered it valuable for teachers to assess student learning at the end of each unit. However, he found that most teachers' classroom assessments did little more than show for whom their initial instruction was and was not appropriate.

A far better approach, according to Bloom, would be for teachers to use their classroom assessments as learning tools, and then to follow those assessments with a *feedback and corrective* procedure. In other words, instead of using assessments only as evaluation devices that mark the end of each unit, Bloom recommended using them as part of the instructional process to *diagnose* individual learning difficulties (feedback) and to *prescribe* remediation procedures (correctives).

This is precisely what takes place when an excellent tutor works with an individual student. If the student makes an error, the tutor first points out the error (feedback), and then follows up with further explanation and clarification (correctives) to ensure the student's understanding. Similarly, academically successful students typically follow up on the mistakes they make on quizzes and assessments. They ask the teacher about the items they missed, look up the answer in the textbook or other resources, or rework the problem or task so that errors are not repeated.

BLOOM'S MASTERY LEARNING

Benjamin Bloom then outlined a specific instructional strategy to make use of this feedback and corrective procedure, labeling it "learning for mastery" (Bloom, 1968), and later shortening the name to simply "mastery learning" (Bloom, 1974). With this strategy, teachers first organize the concepts and skills they want students to learn into instructional units that typically involve about a week or two of instructional time. Following initial instruction on the unit, teachers administer a brief assessment based on the unit's learning goals. Bloom recommended calling this a "formative" assessment, borrowing a term that Scriven (1967) had coined a year earlier to describe the informative, rather than judgmental, aspects of program evaluations. Instead of signifying the end of the unit, this formative assessment's purpose is to give both students and teacher information, or feedback, on each student's learning progress. It helps students and teachers identify specifically what has been learned well to that point and what has not (Bloom, Hastings, & Madaus, 1971).

Paired with each formative assessment are specific "corrective" activities for students to use in correcting their learning difficulties. Most teachers match these correctives to each item or set of prompts within the assessment so that students need work on only those concepts or skills not yet mastered. In other words, the correctives are individualized. They may point out additional sources of information on a particular topic, such as page numbers in the textbook or workbook where the topic is discussed. They may identify alternative learning resources such as different textbooks, learning kits, alternative materials, CDs, videos, or computerized instructional lessons. Or they may simply suggest sources of additional practice, such as study guides, independent or guided practice activities, or collaborative group activities. In most classrooms, teachers direct the corrective activities. But in some, students work independently or in small groups.

With the feedback and corrective information gained from a formative assessment, each student has a detailed prescription of what more needs to be done to master the concepts or skills from the unit. This "just-in-time" correction prevents minor learning difficulties from accumulating and becoming major learning problems. It also gives teachers a practical means to vary and differentiate their instruction in order to better meet students' individual learning needs. As a result, many more students learn well, master the important learning goals in each unit, and gain the necessary prerequisites for success in subsequent units.

The use of "just-in-time" corrections prevents minor learning difficulties from accumulating and becoming major learning problems.

When students complete their corrective activities after a class period or two, Bloom recommended they take a *second* formative assessment. This second, "parallel" assessment covers the same concepts and skills as the first, but is composed of slightly different problems or questions, and serves two important purposes. First, it verifies whether or not the correctives were successful in helping students overcome their individual learning difficulties. Second, it offers students a second chance at success and, hence, has powerful motivational value.

Some students, of course, will perform well on the first assessment, demonstrating that they have mastered the unit concepts and skills. The teacher's initial instruction was highly appropriate for these students, and they have no need of corrective work. To ensure their continued learning progress, Bloom recommended these students be provided with special "enrichment" or "extension" activities to broaden their learning experiences. Such activities often are self-selected by students and might involve special projects or reports, academic games, or a variety of complex problem-solving tasks. Materials designed for gifted and talented students provide an excellent source of enrichment or extension activities. Figure 6.2 illustrates this instructional sequence.

Through this process of formative classroom assessment, combined with the systematic correction of individual learning difficulties,

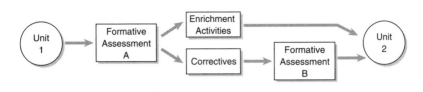

Figure 6.2   The Mastery Learning Instructional Process

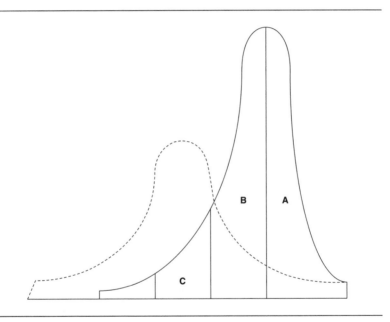

Figure 6.3   Distribution of Achievement in Mastery Learning
Classrooms

Bloom believed all students could be provided with a more appropriate quality of instruction than is possible under more traditional
approaches to teaching. As a result, nearly all might be expected to
learn well and truly master the unit concepts or learning goals (Bloom,
1976). This, in turn, would drastically reduce the variation in students'
achievement levels, eliminate achievement gaps, and yield a distribution of achievement more like that shown in Figure 6.3.

     In describing mastery learning, however, Bloom emphasized
that reducing variation in students' achievement does not imply

making all students the same. Even under these more favorable learning conditions, some students undoubtedly will learn more than others, especially those involved in enrichment activities. But by recognizing relevant, individual differences among students and then altering instruction to better meet their diverse learning needs, Bloom believed the variation among students in terms of how well they learn specific concepts or master a set of articulated learning goals could eventually reach a "vanishing point" (Bloom, 1973). As a result, gaps in the achievement of different groups of students would be closed and all students could be helped to learn excellently.

ESSENTIAL ELEMENTS OF MASTERY LEARNING

After Benjamin Bloom presented his ideas on mastery learning, others described procedures for implementation and numerous programs based on mastery learning principles sprung up in schools and colleges throughout the United States and around the world (e.g., Block, 1971, 1974; Block & Anderson, 1975). While these programs differed from setting to setting, those true to Bloom's ideas included two essential elements: (1) the *feedback, corrective, and enrichment process;* and (2) *instructional alignment* (Guskey, 1997).

Feedback, Correctives, and Enrichment

Teachers who use mastery learning provide students with frequent and specific *feedback* on their learning progress, typically through the use of regular, formative classroom assessments. Furthermore, this feedback is both diagnostic and prescriptive. It reinforces precisely what students were expected to learn, identifies what was learned well, and describes what needs to be learned better. The National Council of Teachers of Mathematics (NCTM) emphasizes this same element in its latest iteration of standards for school mathematics. To overcome inequities in mathematics instruction, NCTM (2000) stresses the use of assessments that support learning and provide useful information to both teachers and students.

Feedback alone, however, does little to help students improve their learning. Significant improvement requires that the feedback be paired with *correctives:* activities that offer guidance and direction to students on how to remedy their learning problems. Because of students' individual differences, no single method of instruction works best for all. To help every student learn well, therefore, teachers must differentiate their instruction, both in their initial teaching and especially through corrective activities (Bloom, 1976). In other words, teachers must *increase* variation in their teaching in order to *decrease* variation in results.

To be optimally effective, correctives must be qualitatively different from the initial teaching. They must provide students who need it with an alternative approach and additional time to learn. The best correctives present concepts differently and involve students in learning differently than did the teacher's initial instruction. They incorporate different learning styles, learning modalities, or types of intelligence. Although developing effective correctives can prove challenging, many schools find that providing teachers with time to work collaboratively, sharing ideas, materials, and expertise, greatly facilitates the process (Guskey, 2001).

Because of students' individual differences, no single method of instruction works best for all. To help every student learn well, teachers must differentiate their instruction.

In most applications of mastery learning, correctives are accompanied by *enrichment* or *extension* activities for students who master the unit concepts from the initial teaching. As described above, enrichment activities offer students exciting opportunities to broaden and expand their learning. They reward students for their learning success but also challenge them to go further. Many teachers draw from activities developed for gifted and talented students when planning enrichment activities, both to simplify implementation tasks and to guarantee these students a high-quality learning experience.

Teachers implement the feedback, corrective, and enrichment process in a variety of ways. Many use short, paper-and-pencil quizzes as formative assessments to give students feedback on their learning progress. But formative assessments also can take the form of essays, compositions, projects, reports, performance tasks, skill demonstrations, oral presentations, or any means used to gain evidence on students' learning progress.

Following a formative assessment, some teachers divide the class into separate corrective and enrichment groups. While the teacher directs corrective activities, guaranteeing that all students with learning difficulties take part, the other students work on self-selected, independent enrichment activities. Other teachers pair with colleagues and use a team-teaching approach. While one teacher oversees corrective activities, the other monitors enrichments. Still other teachers use cooperative learning activities in which students work together in teams to ensure all reach the mastery level. If all attain mastery on the second formative assessment, the entire team receives special recognition or credit.

Feedback, corrective, and enrichment procedures are crucial to mastery learning, for it is through these procedures that mastery learning differentiates and individualizes instruction. In every unit taught, students who need extended time and opportunity to remedy learning problems are offered these through the use of correctives. Those students who learn quickly and for whom the initial instruction was highly appropriate are provided with opportunities to extend their learning through enrichment. As a result, all students are provided with more favorable learning conditions and more appropriate, higher-quality instruction (Bloom, 1977).

Instructional Alignment

While feedback, correctives, and enrichment are extremely important, they alone do not constitute mastery learning. To be truly effective, Bloom stressed they must be combined with the second essential element of mastery learning: *instructional alignment*. Reducing variation in student learning and closing achievement gaps require clarity and consistency among all instructional components.

Most educators see the teaching and learning process as having three major components. To begin with, there must be some idea about what we want students to learn and be able to do—that is, there must be *learning goals or standards*. This is followed by *instruction* that hopefully results in *competent learners*—students who have learned well and whose competence can be gauged through some form of assessment or evaluation. Mastery learning adds the feedback and corrective component, allowing

Reducing variation in student learning and closing achievement gaps require clarity and consistency.

teachers to determine for whom their initial instruction was appropriate and for whom learning alternatives may be needed.

Although essentially neutral with regard to what is taught, how it is taught, and how learning is assessed or evaluated, mastery learning requires consistency or alignment among these instructional components, as shown in Figure 6.4. If, for example, students

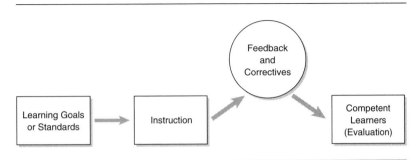

Figure 6.4   Major Components in the Teaching and Learning Process

are expected to learn higher-level skills such as those involved in making applications, problem solving, or analysis, mastery learning stipulates that instructional activities must be planned to give students opportunities to practice and actively engage in those skills. It also requires that students be given specific feedback on how well they have learned those skills, coupled with directions on how to correct any learning errors. Finally, procedures for evaluating students' learning should reflect those higher-level skills as well.

Ensuring alignment among instructional components requires teachers to make several crucial decisions. They must decide, for example, what concepts or skills are most important for students to learn and most central to students' understanding. They also must decide what evidence best reflects students' mastery of those concepts or skills. But, in essence, teachers at all levels make these decisions already. Every time they administer an assessment, grade a paper, or evaluate students' learning, teachers communicate to students what they consider to be most important. Using mastery learning simply compels teachers to make these decisions more thoughtfully and intentionally (see Guskey, 2005).

MISINTERPRETATIONS OF MASTERY LEARNING

Some early attempts to implement mastery learning were based on narrow and inaccurate interpretations of Bloom's ideas. These programs focused on low-level cognitive skills, attempted to break learning down into small segments, and insisted students "master" each segment before being permitted to move on. Teachers were regarded in these programs as little more than managers of materials and record-keepers of student progress.

Nowhere in Bloom's writing can the suggestion of this kind of narrowness and rigidity be found. Bloom always considered thoughtful and reflective teachers vital to the successful implementation of mastery learning and continually stressed flexibility in its application. In his earliest description of the mastery learning process he wrote,

> There are many alternative strategies for mastery learning. Each strategy must find some way of dealing with individual differences in learners through some means of relating instruction to the needs and characteristics of the learners. . . . The alternative high school schedule . . . is one attempt to provide an organizational structure that permits and encourages mastery learning. (Bloom, 1968, pp. 7–8)

Bloom also emphasized the need for instruction in mastery learning classrooms to focus on higher-level learning goals, not simply basic skills. He noted,

> I find great emphasis on problem solving, applications of principles, analytical skills, and creativity. Such higher mental processes are emphasized because this type of learning enables the individual to relate his or her learning to the many problems he or she encounters in day-to-day living. These abilities are stressed because they are retained and utilized long after the individual has forgotten the detailed specifics of the subject matter taught in the schools. These abilities are regarded as one set of essential characteristics needed to continue learning and to cope with a rapidly changing world. (Bloom, 1978, p. 578)

Bloom always considered thoughtful and reflective teachers vital to the successful implementation of mastery learning. He continually stressed the need for flexibility.

Modern research studies show mastery learning to be particularly effective when applied to instruction focusing on higher-level learning goals such as problem solving, drawing inferences, deductive reasoning, and creative expression (Guskey, 1997). The process helps teachers close achievement gaps in a broad range of learning goals, from basic knowledge and skills to highly complex cognitive processes.

In addition, some secondary teachers worry about the constraint of class time. With limited time available, they fear the introduction of feedback, corrective, and enrichment procedures will reduce the amount of content they will be able to cover. As a result, they will have to sacrifice *coverage* for the sake of *mastery*.

The first few mastery learning units typically do require more time than usual. Students must be provided with some orientation to the process, and class time usually needs to be set aside for the teacher to direct students in their corrective work. Teachers who try to have correctives completed as homework or during a special study session before or after school find that those students who most need the extra time are the least likely to take part. As a result, it's not unusual for a mastery learning class to be somewhat behind a more traditionally taught class during the first two or three units.

After students become familiar with the mastery learning process, however, most teachers find that they can pick up the pace of their instruction. Mastery learning students tend to be engaged in learning activities for a larger portion of the time they spend in class. Hence they learn more and learn faster in later units than do students in more traditionally taught classes (Arlin, 1973; Fitzpatrick, 1985). As students catch on to mastery learning, they also tend to do better on first formative assessments. With fewer students involved in correctives and a reduced amount of corrective work required, the class time allocated to correctives in later units can be drastically reduced. Furthermore, because mastery learning students learn well the concepts and skills from early units, they are better prepared for later, more advanced units. This means that less time needs to be spent in review activities. Thus most teachers find that with slight changes in the pacing of their instruction—slightly more time spent in early units but less time in later ones—they are able to cover just as much material as when using more traditional approaches to instruction, and in some cases more (Block, 1983; Guskey, 1983, 1987).

RESEARCH RESULTS

Implementing mastery learning requires relatively modest changes in teachers' instructional procedures. In most cases, it builds on the practices teachers have developed and refined over the years. Most excellent teachers probably use aspects of mastery learning already. Others typically find the process blends well with their present teaching strategies.

Despite the modest nature of these alterations, however, extensive research evidence shows the use of mastery learning can have exceptionally positive effects on student learning. A comprehensive review of the research on mastery learning concluded the following:

> We recently reviewed meta-analyses in nearly 40 different areas of educational research (Kulik & Kulik, 1989). Few educational treatments of any sort were consistently associated with achievement effects as large as those produced by mastery learning. . . . In evaluation after evaluation, mastery programs have produced impressive gains. (Kulik, Kulik, & Bangert-Drowns, 1990, p. 292)

Mastery learning is regularly identified as one of the most effective instructional strategies teachers can employ at any level of education (Walberg, 1984). Some researchers have even suggested that the superiority of Japanese students in international comparisons of achievement in mathematics operations and problem solving may be due largely to the widespread use in Japan of instructional practices similar to mastery learning (Waddington, 1995): providing feedback, correctives, and enrichments; and ensuring that instructional alignment takes relatively little time and effort, especially if tasks are shared collaboratively among teaching colleagues. Results have shown that the systematic use of these elements helps many more students learn well, significantly reduces variation in student learning outcomes, and closes gaps in the achievement of different groups of students.

Mastery learning is regularly identified as one of the most effective instructional strategies teachers can employ at any level of education.

Equally important, the positive effects of mastery learning are evident not only in measures of student achievement. The process also has been shown to yield improvements in students' confidence in learning situations, school attendance rates, involvement in class lessons, attitudes toward learning, and a host of other affective measures (Guskey & Pigott, 1988). This multidimensional impact has been referred to as the "multiplier effect" of mastery learning, and makes it an especially powerful tool in school improvement efforts.

Conclusion

Numerous factors affect student learning, many lying beyond class-room walls and outside of teachers' control. A recent Educational Testing Service report, for example, identified a wide range of environmental factors that may contribute to achievement gaps, the majority of which are external to schools (Barton, 2003). Denying the role of these outside influences will not endow teachers and schools with the capacity to reduce achievement gaps, and efforts to address these home- and community-based challenges must continue (Rothstein, 2004). Nevertheless, the impediments to learning that come from students' environments outside of school should never become a basis for lowering expectations about what can be done to help them learn well in school.

The feedback, correctives, and enrichment process, as well as the instructional alignment elements of mastery learning, represent powerful tools that teachers can use to capitalize on the influence they have. They are not, of course, the only factors of importance. In his later writing, Bloom described exciting work on other ideas designed to attain results even more positive than those typically achieved with mastery learning, labeling this the "two-sigma challenge" (Bloom, 1984a, 1984b, 1988). Still, careful attention to these elements allows educators at all levels to make great strides in their efforts to reduce variation in student achievement and close achievement gaps. They offer the tools educators need to help *all* students learn excellently, including those of different racial, ethnic, and socioeconomic backgrounds. As a result of utilizing these tools, many more students will learn excellently, succeed in school, and gain the many positive benefits that come from that success.

References

Arlin, M. N. (1973). *Rate and rate variance trends under mastery learning.* Unpublished doctoral dissertation, University of Chicago.

Barton, P. E. (2003). *Parsing the achievement gap: Baselines for traking progress* (Policy information report). Princeton, NJ: Educational Testing Service.

Block, J. H. (Ed.). (1971). *Mastery learning: Theory and practice.* New York: Holt, Rinehart & Winston.

Block, J. H. (Ed.). (1974). *Schools, society, and mastery learning.* New York: Holt, Rinehart & Winston.

Block, J. H. (1983). Learning rates and mastery learning. *Outcomes, 2*(3), 18–23.

Block, J. H., & Anderson, L. W. (1975). *Mastery learning in classroom instruction.* New York: MacMillan.

Bloom, B. S. (1964). *Stability and change in human characteristics.* New York: Wiley.

Bloom, B. S. (1968). Learning for mastery. *Evaluation Comment, 1*(2), 1–12.

Bloom, B. S. (1973). Individual differences in school achievement: A vanishing point? In L. J. Rubin (Ed.), *Facts and feelings in the classroom.* New York: Walker.

Bloom, B. S. (1974). An introduction to mastery learning theory. In J. H. Block (Ed.), *Schools, society, and mastery learning.* New York: Holt, Rinehart & Winston.

Bloom, B. S. (1976). *Human characteristics and school learning.* New York: McGraw-Hill.

Bloom, B. S. (1977). Favorable learning conditions for all. *Teacher, 95*(3), 22–28.

Bloom, B. S. (1978). New views of the learner: Implications for instruction and curriculum. *Educational Leadership, 35*(7), 563–576.

Bloom, B. S. (1984a). The 2 sigma problem: The search for methods of group instruction as effective as one-to-one tutoring. *Educational Researcher, 13*(6), 4–16.

Bloom, B. S. (1984b). The search for methods of group instruction as effective as one-to-one tutoring. *Educational Leadership, 41*(8), 4–17.

Bloom, B. S. (1988). Helping all children learn in elementary school and beyond. *Principal, 67*(4), 12–17.

Bloom, B. S., Hastings, J. T., & Madaus, G. (1971). *Handbook on formative and summative evaluation of student learning.* New York: McGraw-Hill.

Dollard, J., & Miller, N. E. (1950). *Personality and psychotherapy.* New York: McGraw-Hill.

Fitzpatrick, K. A. (1985). *Group-based mastery learning: A Robin Hood approach to instruction?* Paper presented at the annual meeting of the American Educational Research Association, Chicago.

Guskey, T. R. (1983). Clarifying time related issues. *Outcomes, 3*(1), 5–7.

Guskey, T. R. (1987). Rethinking mastery learning reconsidered. *Review of Educational Research, 57*(2), 225–229.

Guskey, T. R. (1997). *Implementing mastery learning* (2nd ed.). Belmont, CA: Wadsworth.

Guskey, T. R. (2001). Mastery learning. In N. J. Smelser & P. B. Baltes (Eds.), *International encyclopedia of social and behavioral sciences* (pp. 9372–9377). Oxford, England: Elsevier Science.

Guskey, T. R. (2005). Mapping the road to proficiency. *Educational Leadership, 63*(3), 32–38.

Guskey, T. R. (Ed.). (2006). *Benjamin S. Bloom: Portraits of an educator.* Lanham, MD: Rowman & Littlefield Education.

Guskey, T. R., & Pigott, T. D. (1988). Research on group-based mastery learning programs: A meta-analysis. *Journal of Educational Research, 81*(4), 197–216.

Kulik, C. C., Kulik, J. A., & Bangert-Drowns, R. L. (1990). Effectiveness of mastery learning programs: A meta-analysis. *Review of Educational Research, 60*(2), 265–299.

Kulik, J. A., & Kulik, C. C. (1989). Meta-analysis in education. *International Journal of Educational Research, 13*(2), 221–340.

Morrison, H. C. (1926). *The practice of teaching in the secondary school.* Chicago: University of Chicago Press.

National Council of Teachers of Mathematics. (2000). *Principles and standards for school mathematics.* Reston, VA: Author. Available: http://standards.nctm.org/document/index.htm

Rothstein, R. (2004). A wider lens on the black-white achievement gap. *Phi Delta Kappan, 86*(2), 104–110.

Scriven, M. (1967). The methodology of evaluation. In R. W. Tyler, R. M. Gagne, & M. Scriven (Eds.), *Perspectives of curriculum evaluation* (pp. 39–83). AERA Monograph Series on Curriculum Evaluation, No. 1. Chicago: Rand McNally.

Waddington, T. (1995). *Why mastery matters.* Paper presented at the annual meeting of the American Educational Research Association, San Francisco.

Walberg, H. J. (1984). Improving the productivity of America's schools. *Educational Leadership, 41*(8), 19–27.

Washburne, C. W. (1922). Educational measurements as a key to individualizing instruction and promotions. *Journal of Educational Research, 5,* 195–206.

CHAPTER SEVEN

ENGAGING EVERY LEARNER

Blurring the Lines for
Learning to Ensure That All Young
People Are Ready for College, Work, and Life

KAREN J. PITTMAN AND MERITA IRBY

U niversal access to public education is a fundamental right in America—a right that many assume comes with a promise of equal quality and adequate, if not equal, progress. But the one-two punch delivered by the application of the federal requirements of No Child Left Behind to high school graduation (U.S. Department of Education, 2003) and the widely publicized recalculations of high school graduation rates has created a newfound sense of urgency among policy makers and the public. Data from the Manhattan Institute and others suggest that nationally only two-thirds of all entering ninth graders graduate within four years, and that the odds of an on-time graduation in many urban areas are about 50–50 (Campaign for Youth, 2005; Greene & Winters, 2005; National Governors Association, 2005; Swanson, 2004).

These numbers are sobering enough, but they do not tell the full story. There is growing concern from youth workers, employers, and college administrators that a significant fraction of those young people who graduate are not fully prepared for work, post-secondary education, or the basic demands of adulthood (Baer, Cook, & Baldi, 2006; Colorado Commission on Higher Education, 2005).

Sophisticated analyses of several longitudinal data sets that tracked young people from their early teens into their early twenties suggest that only 4 out of 10 young people are doing well as young adults—productive (in college or working), healthy (physically, socially, and emotionally), and/or connected (to a community or cause larger than themselves). Two out of 10 are in serious trouble (Gambone, Klem, & Connell, 2002). This landmark study further suggests that these odds could be improved significantly if *all* teens had access to the basic supports that only some teens had during their high school years: safe environments, supportive relationships, challenging learning experiences, and opportunities to be recognized and make meaningful contributions.

Only 4 out of 10 young people are doing well as young adults. Two out of 10 are in serious trouble.

The authors, Gambone, Klem, and Connell, suggest that by simply ensuring a steady dose of supports, these odds could change to 7 out of 10 doing well and only 1 out of 10 doing badly.

States and communities can change the odds for young people to ensure that significantly more are ready for college, work, and life. Doing so, however, requires making fundamental changes in the ways they do business—how they define the problems; what they identify as the solutions; when, how, and where they begin to make changes; and whom they enlist as key change makers. There is no more relevant place to begin making these fundamental changes than with the prevailing assumptions about education and school reform. Why? Two reasons:

- *Learning does not end inside the classroom.* Engaging *all* students in achieving high academic standards requires commitments to increase rigor, relevance, and relationships—the new three Rs. Making good on these commitments, in turn, requires deeper partnerships with a wide range of organizations outside of the school boundaries. This will not only bring "context" into the classroom, but it will also invite students into spaces in which they are trained and expected to deliver against timelines and standards that have real consequences associated with failure and real rewards associated with success. This is as true for the college-ready as it is for the ill-prepared. Site visits and simulations are simply not the same as the real thing.

- *Not all of our students are staying inside the classroom.* As noted, fully one-third of all ninth graders drop out of school by twelfth grade. Of those who stay, many are present in body but absent in mind and spirit. It is both possible and necessary to hold our state and local education systems accountable for ensuring that "all youth are ready." But it is not feasible to think this goal will be accomplished by pushing young people back into contact with the structures and staff that have failed them. New solutions must be found.

The Forum for Youth Investment is a nonpartisan "action tank" devoted to developing innovative ideas, strategies, and partnerships to strengthen solutions for young people and those who care about them (www.forumfyi.org). Ready by 21™ is the Forum's synthesis of years of rigorous research and practical experience in focusing national attention on optimizing resources and streamlining strategies to ensure that every young person is "Ready by 21"—ready for college, work, and life. As cofounders of the Forum, we strongly believe that education and educators are at the core of both the problems *and* the solutions. We are equally adamant, however, that decisions about when, how, where, why, and for whom change should be made and implemented should be youth-focused and community-based. This chapter lays out the arguments behind this vision.

THE CALL FOR COMMUNITY EDUCATION PARTNERSHIPS

The Community Partnerships strategy is based on a radical approach to improving educational opportunities in a city. It acknowledges that the traditional boundaries between the public school system's responsibilities and those of other community agencies are themselves part of the educational problem ... the strategy opens new options for education, asking "How can this community use all its assets to provide the best education for all our children?" The Community Partnerships strategy would include multiple public and private providers. It would in addition be a genuine community-wide system in that all the community's resources, not simply its schools, would be available in an organized way to meet children's educational needs and their general well being. (Hill, Campbell, & Harvey, 2000, p. 76)

Paul Hill and his colleagues have studied successful school reform efforts in numerous cities, looking for commonalities, gaps, and clues. Their conclusion, and the title of their book, is that it takes a city to educate children. Their boldest proposal for reforming K–12 education is to create community partnerships that tap into and organize the full array of educational resources available in communities—in libraries, museums, faith-based institutions, community-based organizations, and nonprofits. Beyond their responsibility for contracting for publicly funded schools, these partnerships would "encourage nonschool educational resources" to enrich the schools' curriculum, leverage public and private dollars for community-based organizations in order to "preserve a portfolio of educational alternatives for the disadvantaged," and "broker health and social service resources to meet children's needs" (Hill, Campbell, & Harvey, 2000, pp. 77–78).

"The school is not and cannot be an institution apart. Nor is it, nor can it be, the exclusive provider in a community's educational system."

—John Goodlad

The authors of *It Takes a City* reinforce the fact that there are numerous community resources that can and should be enlisted to support young people's education and development. They make two distinct but complementary points: These institutions can help strengthen learning during the school day, and they have the power to reinforce learning and contributions in the many hours when young people are with their families and friends and in their neighborhoods.

Hill and his colleagues are ahead of many in proposing that boards of education be replaced by bold new community partnerships charged not with maintaining schools, but with promoting communitywide supports for learning. They are anything but alone, however, in their conclusion that what exists for young people outside of the school building matters enormously. Nor are they alone in arguing that it will take communitywide commitments to learning—blurring the lines to connect learning experiences inside and outside of the school day and the school building—in order to ensure that young people are problem free, fully prepared, and fully engaged.

The nation's leading education reformers have been making similar arguments for more than two decades:

> The school is not and cannot be an institution apart. Nor is it, nor can it be, the exclusive provider in a community's educational system. . . . The school may be the only institution charged exclusively with the educational function, but the ability and responsibility of others to educate is recognized and cultivated. There is not one agency, but an ecology of institutions educating— school, home, places of worship, television, press, museums, libraries, businesses, factories and more. (Goodlad, 1984)

More than ever, schools and districts seem ready to act on these proposals—while recognizing that there is serious work involved in implementing such a vision:

> I think it's a real challenge for cities to get to the point where they can claim a coordinated effort in supporting kids' out-of-school and in-school learning. That's the goal that people should try to reach—but it's not easy. That takes infrastructure, and also a common framework. Without the framework, it ends up being piecemeal, or there are gaps. Without a common dialog and frameworks across school and community, and among community interests, things just remain fragmented. (T. Del Prete, personal communication, December 2001)

Perhaps most important, young people themselves are looking for ways to weave together learning experiences in and out of school. In particular, high school students whose schools and organizations blur these boundaries speak compellingly of their educational experiences:

> My school is called School Without Walls. A big part of our school's philosophy is that we use the community as a classroom, which means we have a partnership with George Washington University. At our school, we have maybe 20 classrooms. We have no auditorium. We have no gym. We have no lockers. We have no playing field. We have none of that. We use all of GW's, and it makes our students much more resourceful in the way that they go about things. We use a lot of museums.

We use GW's facilities. I think it makes people in our school a lot more independent and focused. And, with a block schedule, we have more time to go to museums, to sit down and listen to all the audio-visuals inside the museums.

Another thing that makes my school work: At other schools there seems to be a lot of competition between the after-school program and the school near the end of the school day when programs want the students to go out in the community and do other things. That partnership at my school is a lot stronger than at other schools. Instead of the afterschool program fighting to get students let out 15 minutes early so that they can be at their internship on time, there's give-and-take between community partners and schools.

I think the reason why I like the schedule is because our school is humanities-based. We always have a connection back to reality, back to life, back to the other disciplines inside the school. That makes a big difference. If you don't have something tying it all together, it just seems like you're going to eight different teachers, learning eight different lessons. (Tolman, 2000)

We quote Delonte at such length because his words contain all the critical elements of the vision we are advancing. Schools have always had functional partnerships with nonprofit organizations, businesses, and public service agencies that can supplement school personnel and resources and, in some cases, take advantage of school facilities. Any effective school principal can provide a long list of partners. But what Delonte describes is far richer and more expansive than what exists in most schools. Community resources have become a critical part of learning during the school day itself. In-school learning experiences push the boundaries of the school day, so that young people have time for deeper, more deliberate experiences. School-based learning experiences are connected with those that take place in community organizations; there is a "give and take," a recognition that both serve important and linked functions. In the process, the learning experience inside the school day and school building is transformed—and genuine, deep, and lasting school reform occurs. Let us look at the parts of this vision one at a time.

Community resources have become a critical part of learning during the school day itself.

To enrich students' learning opportunities during the school day, schools are forming partnerships with businesses, colleges and universities, artists and craftspeople, health and social service agencies, and nonprofits to bring additional expertise and services into the school building and to offer students off-campus opportunities for learning, work, service, and preventive supports. In some cases, these partners are delegated primary responsibility for academic education through charters or have assumed responsibility for educating students who have dropped out (The Forum for Youth Investment, 2004a) (Figure 7.1, Box 1).

To create additional opportunities for learning, especially for those who have fallen behind, schools are also moving beyond traditional commitments to provide extracurricular activities and summer schooling to house, if not provide, formal afterschool programs for students, particularly those in the elementary grades. This trend builds on educators' desires to address students' remedial needs as well as respond to parents' needs for afterschool care. There is no doubt, however, that it has been facilitated by an infusion of one billion new federal dollars through the 21st Century Community Learning Centers Program, coupled with ambitious state efforts such as those undertaken in California and Massachusetts (Afterschool Investments Project, 2005; The Forum for Youth Investment, 2003a; Naughton & Teare, 2005) (Figure 7.1, Box 2).

To build alignment and connections with the other places where students learn, schools are creating stronger partnerships with a broad array of organizations that offer formal and informal opportunities for learning and engagement. These partners include youth-serving organizations, civic and human services nonprofits, faith-based organizations, recreation departments, libraries, museums, businesses, and others, supported by public and private dollars. These organizations complement schools' focus on academic competence by providing opportunities for civic, social, physical, vocational and spiritual supports, learning, and engagement. Increasingly, they are not only sharing space with schools, but also receiving referrals and creating joint ventures such as community schools (Blank, Melaville, & Shah, 2003; Coalition for Community Schools Web site; The Forum for Youth Investment, 2003b, 2004b, 2005) (Figure 7.1, Box 3).

To better fulfill their core commitment to support student academic achievement, schools are building more connected and aligned learning experiences within the school day—through new forms

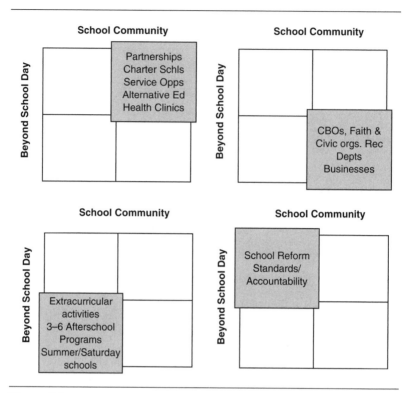

Figure 7.1

of accountability, as well as efforts to integrate curriculum and shift instruction. The standards movement has, in many ways, artificially narrowed the definition of "learning," causing educators to focus their energy on the reading and math skills for which they are held accountable and, even more dangerously, on improvements in the standardized tests that purport to measure success. But it has also resulted in a new openness. Schools recognize that they cannot go it alone—that more time and resources are necessary in order to meet higher standards, and that they will need not only the political support, but the day-to-day help of families, businesses, community organizations, and other educational institutions. This is particularly true at the high school level, where it is increasingly clear that creating environments

> *Schools recognize that they cannot go it alone—that more time and resources are necessary in order to meet higher standards.*

in which young people feel safe, known, and respected is a precondition to learning. This fact has created a new willingness to see youth development professionals as experts (The Forum for Youth Investment, 2003c; Jobs for the Future, 2002; Pittman & Tolman, 2002) (Figure 7.1, Box 4).

The most critical element of the vision, however, is the ongoing interaction between these four quadrants of learning (Figure 7.2). These connections are critical for individual young people; they provide the space to expand and explore the broader who, what, where, when, how, and why of learning. They allow young people to see disparate learning experiences as part of a larger whole. They create the temporal, spatial, and transactional opportunities to simultaneously achieve "rigor, relevance, and relationships"—the current mantra of high school reform (Bill and Melinda Gates Foundation, n.d.; Council of Chief State School Officers & The Forum for Youth Investment, 2001).

It is even more important that these connections be understood, explained, and supported at the community level, where shared accountability for learning outcomes, consistent community-wide engagement and commitment, compatible definitions of effective learning environments, and ongoing ways to ensure alignment and connection are becoming critical issues of the 21st century.

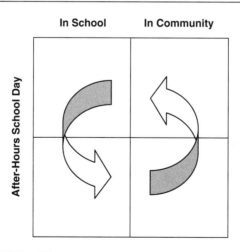

Figure 7.2

The challenges involved in building these types of cross-sector, cross-system connections at the community level are enormous, to say the least. Calls for collaboration and coordination are far more common than concrete results. It is not only fair but important to ask, "Why bother?"

WHY COMMUNITY EDUCATION PARTNERSHIPS ARE CRITICAL

There is broad agreement that all young people need to be fully prepared to be workers, citizens, and parents, and there has come to be general recognition that family and community resources beyond school play a role in their preparation. But if actions reflect beliefs, the dominant sentiment is that these partners are nice but not necessary: K–12 school systems are the core of the learning equation and until they are fixed, nothing else will matter. There is some truth to this argument. Proponents of after-school programs, for example, have fought hard to be measured against a set of metrics that are not centered on improving academic achievement, arguing that they should not be expected to do in a few hours what the school is unable to accomplish in a full day.

Not all learning happens in the classroom and not all students are in the classroom.

In reality, the combination of the two realities noted at the beginning of this paper—not all learning happens in the classroom, and not all students are *in* the classroom—coincides with rapidly growing evidence that there are real, viable options for extending the responsibility for formal, rigorous learning beyond the temporal, staff, and structural boundaries of the traditional school. Public legislation and private funding have cultivated an unprecedented growth of new schools (small schools, charter schools), frequently created and staffed by new partners (community colleges, nonprofit organizations). Some of these "alternative" institutions are demonstrating better retention, promotion, and college-going rates than "traditional" high schools. Equally important, an expansion in community ownership of formal education responsibilities has been accompanied by an equal, if not greater, accountability for ensuring that middle and high school students have a range of informal learning opportunities (e.g., the Afterschool and Community Schools movements).

These advances in "blurring the lines" between school and community build on and reinforce several other lessons that have been learned:

- Academic competence, while critical, is not enough. Critical outcomes span a range of functional areas, pushing beyond academic knowledge or cognitive development to encompass broader moral, physical, civic, social, and vocational goals. This is the bigger picture of learning and engagement on which it is important to focus: all young people who are problem free, fully prepared, and fully engaged across a range of basic functional areas. Research has identified the broad range of assets needed for adolescent and adult success. The public has affirmed the importance of a broader set of "21st century skills" and expressed concern about students' lack of preparation in these areas as well as in the basics. And students themselves are concerned about the gaps (America's Promise, 2005; National Research Council & Institute of Medicine, 2004; Partnership for 21st Century Skills, 2003) (Figure 7.3).

- School, while it must be the hub of learning, does not have enough spokes to meet the diverse learning and engagement needs of all students. Especially by high school, students need more time, more people, and more places. Schools do not have the capacity, on their own, to ensure that all young people are prepared for the transition to careers, citizenship, and family and community life. They cannot and should not be the only learning organization in young people's lives. From a time perspective, schools fill at best a quarter of young people's waking hours. From a mandate perspective, schools have primary responsibility for academic learning, not for the full range of areas in which young people need to be learning and engaged. Schools need community learning partners to recapture those who have left, reignite those who have tuned out or given up, and reinforce those who are on the right track.

- The public wants institutional and outcome accountability. Schools are only one of a range of learning environments that share responsibility for helping students learn and achieve mastery. Community-based organizations, museums, libraries, parks, workplaces, community health centers, families, and so forth are not simply places to keep young people safe when they are not in school or providers of basic services that ensure young people are ready to learn. They are also settings for learning and engagement, appropriately

Physical development

- Good health habits
- Good health risk-management skills

Intellectual development

- Knowledge of essential life skills
- Knowledge of essential vocational skills
- School success
- Rational habits of mind—critical thinking and reasoning skills
- In-depth knowledge of more than one culture
- Good decision-making skills
- Knowledge of skills needed to navigate through multiple cultural contexts

Psychological and emotional development

- Good mental health including positive self-regard
- Good emotional self-regulation skills
- Good coping skills
- Good conflict-resolution skills
- Mastery motivation and positive achievement motivation
- Confidence in one's personal efficacy
- "Planfulness"–planning for the future and future life events
- Sense of personal autonomy/responsibility for self
- Optimism coupled with realism
- Coherent and positive personal and social identity
- Pro-social and culturally sensitive values
- Spirituality or a sense of a "larger" purpose in life
- Strong moral character
- A commitment to good use of time

Social development

- Connectedness—perceived good relationships and trust with parents, peers, and some other adults
- Sense of social place/integration—being connected to and valued by larger social networks
- Attachment to pro-social/conventional institutions, such as school, church, non-school youth programs
- Ability to navigate in multiple cultural contexts
- Commitment to civic engagement

Figure 7.3   Personal and Social Assets That Facilitate Positive Youth Development

(From the National Research Council & Institute of Medicine, *Community Programs to Promote Youth Development,* 2002.)

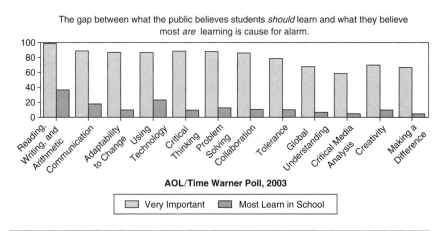

Figure 7.4   Percentage Who Believe 21st Century Skills Are Important With Percentage Who Believe Most Students Learn Skills in School

focusing on issues connected to but beyond academic success. That said, the public is not interested in decentralizing learning. Polling suggests that while the public wants young people to have a broader menu of learning options in order to develop a broader set of competencies (Figure 7.4), it still wants schools to be accountable (Figure 7.5)—because schools have the resources, the mandate, and the authority to coordinate learning. Strong beliefs that young people need a broad range of skills are correlated with strong beliefs that schools should somehow expand their mandate (The Forum for Youth Investment, 2003c; Time Warner Foundation, 2003).

• Research supports the development of definitions and assessments of program quality and student competence that can be applied across settings. Not only is there broad general agreement about the skills and competencies young people need, there is also growing agreement about what it takes to ensure that young people have the opportunities they need to be fully prepared and engaged. The National Research Council has done the nation an enormous service in reviewing the research across fields and compiling a generic chart on the characteristics of effective settings for learning and development (Figure 7.6). This important report not only lists the characteristics, it also defines the ends of the continua, describing practices that

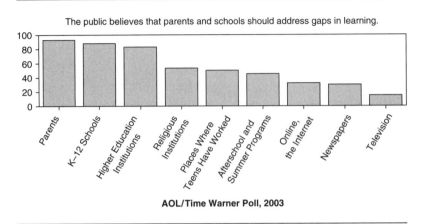

AOL/Time Warner Poll, 2003

Figure 7.5   Individuals and Organizations Important for Learning

can do harm, as well as those that do good. The supports, services, and opportunities that young people need in order to attain the goals associated with productive adulthood reflect critical components identified again and again in the literature and validated by the National Research Council as being the signs of a quality learning environment—whether the setting is a classroom, a sports team, a youth center, or an employment program (National Research Council & Institute of Medicine, 2002; Pittman & Yohalem, 2002).

Equally important, this agreement about universal definitions of program quality and youth outcomes is driving a quest for setting-neutral assessments. The Partnership for 21st Century Skills, for example, is investing in the documentation and development of 21st-century assessments that measure progress in the key skill areas (Partnership for 21st Century Skills, 2005). The High/Scope Educational Research Foundation has developed a well-researched program quality assessment tool that is being used by schools systems, youth organizations, and public youth services providers (High/Scope Educational Research Foundation, n.d.; Yohalem, Wilson-Ahlstrom, & Yu, 2005).

Research also demonstrates the utility of providing all young people with multiple settings for learning and engagement, but doing so especially for those with learning challenges. While the core characteristics of effective learning environments are similar across settings, learning experiences outside the school day and the school

The Forum for Youth Investment's work with 11 school districts in California to help create school–community partnerships for high school reform and student success underscored the need to identify and implement effective educational improvement strategies with these other key tasks. Interviews with the school and community partners in each district (who each received small staffing grants to facilitate their work together) netted these lessons:

- Community partners (organizations that play catalytic roles in asessing community capacity, convening stakeholders, interfacing with district leaders, etc.) are critical for generating and sustaining momentum for the change process.
- Separate funding streams for district and community partners are essential in developing a balance of power and establishing equity in the working relationship.
- Technical assistance is useful when it comes in the form of flexible, customized coaching and networking and resource identification. The key is a focus not just on school improvement strategies but on strategies that help communities tackle the larger challenges of shaping a common vision and engaging all stakeholders.
- Youth engagement is important. Explicitly challenging districts and communities to engage young people and families in the planning process forced rethinking of assumptions and improved the plans.
- External incentives create the climate for change, but flexibility in the planning process was critical for getting buy-in and building momentum. It is important not to have prescriptions imposed. It was equally important, however, that the external request was for a plan, not a proposal.

Figure 7.6   Building Community Education Partnerships: The California Experience

(From Joselowsky & Yohalem, *District/Community Alliances to Transform Schools: Lessons Learned from California's High School Pupil Success Act,* 2005.)

building offer an important complement to those based in schools. Research suggests that students are more likely to be engaged—cognitively and emotionally—in learning environments outside of school (see Figure 7.7) (Larson, 2000). This does not mean that schools should close and accountability be shifted to more informal learning settings. It does suggest, however, that nonschool environments, working in partnership with schools, are perhaps the most effective settings to build nonacademic skills for career and life and to reengage students who have disengaged from school. It also means that other learning environments—that have to attract and retain participants voluntarily—have something to teach public school educators, and that building connections between schools and

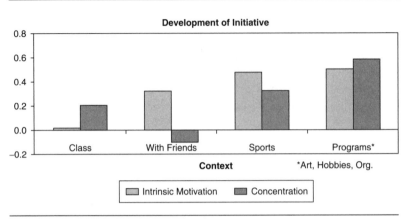

Figure 7.7
(From Reed Larson, *American Psychologist,* January 2000.)

community-based learning partners is likely to improve the quality of instruction inside schools.

WHY COMMUNITY EDUCATION PARTNERSHIPS ARE DIFFICULT

There is nothing easy about the task of building a strong community partnership to ensure that all young people are learning. It requires the management and alignment of at least three and probably four overlapping major change efforts to (1) improve public education, (2) increase informal out-of-school learning opportunities (expand afterschool, extended learning, or extra learning programs), (3) address the needs of out-of-school teens and young adults, and (4) increase public demand and cross-system accountability for improved youth outcomes.

The first three categories of change efforts are focused on building or improving broad service-delivery systems that, combined, promise to provide young people with the supports needed to be ready for college, work, and life and to make successful transitions from high school. The fourth category reflects the growing concern that, without aggressive management, multiple change efforts can confuse the public and policy makers, compete for attention and dollars, and increase services without increasing results because no one is watching the Big Picture.

The challenges differ enormously in size and scope for those reforming schools versus those transforming community learning opportunities in the out-of-school hours or for out-of-school youth. So, too, do the financial, policy, and institutional resources involved with each and, to some extent, the specific populations targeted. But the challenges center around the same issues: redefining and improving practice, strengthening the capacity of those who teach and lead, creating structures and policies that support rather than thwart student learning and ground-level leadership, and maintaining public and political will.

It is clear that, at the end of the day, there must be bridges between the formal educational system and the more informal community learning systems that support out-of-school time and out-of-school youth.

It is clear that, at the end of the day, there must be bridges between the formal educational system and the more informal community learning opportunities systems that support out-of-school time and out-of-school youth. These systems are like metropolitan areas that connect several cities (sometimes across state lines) and have interlocking economies that require cross-city negotiations on issues ranging from transportation to human services to tax policies. And, like these areas, there comes a point when coexistence becomes complex enough that it is important to consider formalizing the connections. Three questions are worth asking:

1. Should these challenges be tackled together? Is there reason to believe that outcomes would be better if schools and community actors planned and trained together or at least were informed by each other's work?

2. Can these challenges be tackled together? Are the differences in mission, size, budget, structure, and accountability simply too great, even if the reasons for connecting are valid?

3. Have these challenges been tackled together? Are there examples of cities in which the school district and the community have come together to forge joint responses?

These are serious questions that deserve serious answers—a task that is beyond the scope of this chapter. We would argue, based on what we know, that the answers are (1) absolutely, (2) with difficulty, and (3) in a few places.

Should the systems work together? Absolutely. We have already explained many of the reasons why this connection is vital. The language is different, but the changes in practices being discussed in school reform parallel closely the practices that are being encouraged and codified in the out-of-school learning arena. Practices such as team teaching, project-based learning, student advisories, and block classes all have counterparts in the more informal learning environments created by alternative schools, nonprofit youth organizations, museums, community recreation centers, and faith institutions. Resource and requirement levels are different, but both systems are struggling to make inservice training more relevant, to create better environments for supervision and peer support, to link performance to pay, and to revamp (or create) preservice credentialing. And at the leadership levels, it is difficult to imagine how changes will be sustained if policies are not agreed to and institutionalized across systems.

One of the most logical and important places for in-school and out-of-school systems to join forces is in the areas of training and staffing.

Can the systems work together? With difficulty. Sharing space would seem to be a straightforward process, yet even this task has raised legitimate concerns about liabilities, facilities overuse, and shared costs. One of the most logical and important places for the systems to join forces is around training and staffing. Yet these will probably be some of the most contentious issues to tackle. Teachers and youth workers have different pay scales, benefits, contracts, and very different bargaining power. Even in cities without strong teachers' unions, debates over who provides the programming can cripple expansion efforts because of the cost of hiring tenured teachers versus part-time youth workers. At the leadership level, principals and program directors have to deal with the fact that the principal has the lion's share of power. This is exacerbated even more at the district level, where the superintendent does not have a counterpart unless the city has created not just a task force, but a fully authorized, fully accountable department that handles all public dollars related to community programming for children and youth.

Beneath the question of coordinating training and staffing, however, lies another of the challenges associated with forging effective community education partnerships: bringing together stakeholders without starting battles over turf. Each of the systems and sectors associated with a strong partnership will have its own way of doing business. Uniting them under a common "big picture" vision for the youth they serve will require that they understand the need to change the way they do their business—at least in part—and this is no mean feat. Done incorrectly, such effort can trigger territoriality and intransigence. However, if not done at all, the answer is clear: discordant systems leading to young people insufficiently prepared for the challenges of college, work, and life.

Have these systems worked together? Yes, here and there. While mayors in general are still reluctant to step into K–12 school reform with both feet, a growing number of mayors and governors are making the afterschool hours and, in some instances, the broader alternative pathways/out-of-school youth issues their own. (The National League of Cities has significant technical assistance projects underway in both areas.) Mayors and superintendents in cities such as Providence, Nashville, Boston, and New York are working together to create joint initiatives, integrated systems, or linked services. The Beacon Schools, one of the premier examples of effective community schools, was started as a partnership between the New York City mayor's office, the school district, and community organizations, and has been taken to scale in New York and replicated across the country. The mayor and the superintendent in Boston have worked closely in creating literacy programs that blur the school-community lines. Several of the districts participating in the Carnegie Corporation/Gates Foundation Schools for a New Society Initiative have ambitious plans for linking school and community learning opportunities through joint planning, training, and programming.

WHY COMMUNITY CATALYSTS ARE NEEDED

The time is right to create strong public-private partnerships and to leverage a sustained commitment to community-wide learning and engagement that is as unwavering as the country's current commitment to traditional K–12 education. Furthermore, this commitment must link to public education through a bold new definition of learning that reflects youth and community members' broader definitions of the who, what, where, when, why, and how of learning.

The hours between 9 AM and 3 PM are the focal point of this country's public commitment to learning. Every child is entitled to a K–12 public education that prepares him or her for post-secondary education, work, and citizenship. Annually, states and localities spend an average of $8,259 per student on public education—for instruction that runs six to seven hours per day, 180 days per year (National Center for Educational Statistics, 2004).

The time is right to create strong public-private partnerships and to leverage a sustained commitment to community-wide learning that is as unwavering as our current commitment to traditional K–12 education.

Two decades of school reform work have netted significant progress. School districts galvanized by clearer academic goals and lines of accountability have moved test scores and begun to close persistent achievement gaps. Targeted efforts to reduce class and school size, recruit better-qualified teachers, and refocus on higher academic standards have resulted in genuine, measurable improvements in student learning. Major public and private initiatives—while not equally successful in every city—have resulted in improved schools in some of the nation's largest and traditionally lowest-performing districts. Just as important, these efforts have focused the nation's attention on urban schools. The question will never again be whether to invest in these schools, but how to best target that investment.

But these efforts have fallen short, and will continue to do so. Why? Because schools cannot go it alone. However diverse their strategies and targets, school reform efforts are only a piece of what is needed in education reform. Learning is a community matter—something that goes on outside the school building as much as inside its confines, outside the school day as much as between 8 AM and 3 PM. Unless schools are embedded in communities rich in learning opportunities and supports, unless communities as a whole have committed themselves to quality education for all their young people, schools cannot hope to succeed. That is the challenge before us: a community challenge.

Each of the three overlapping delivery systems (K–12 education, afterschool, second chance/vulnerable youth) has internal work to do to improve the quality, quantity, and continuity of what is offered by increasing the capacity to provide technical supports and securing and distributing funding. But in the end, there is a larger set of tasks that have to be accomplished that are best tackled by the community rather than by the individual systems:

- Creating a shared, actionable vision for student success that is youth-focused, rather than system-focused, anchored by grounded definitions of the skills and competencies young people need to succeed in adulthood and the opportunities, services, and supports they need to achieve these outcomes.

- Increasing youth, parent, and teacher involvement—from young people, parents, and community members—is essential to the long-term sustainability of any effort, especially one that will ultimately require reallocation of public funds and/or redefinition of public priorities.

- Securing broad stakeholder engagement and accountability by creating a "big tent" agenda in which high school reform is presented as the central ingredient of a larger community-wide effort. This effort should look to ensure that young people graduate from high school ready for the next task by identifying other opportunities for community contribution and setting clear objectives for which there is public monitoring and shared accountability.

- Assessing and aligning public and private policies, practices, and funding to reduce fragmentation and ensure maximum returns on all investments.

The Forum's work with state and community leaders across the country has led us to conclude that these cross-cutting tasks cannot be done by the individual systems that are busy with internal reforms and restructuring efforts. (For example, see sidebar on lessons learned by 11 California school districts' efforts to build school-community partnerships for high school reform.) Silo systems often require the creation of an overarching body whose primary purpose is to "monitor, manage, and message" the Big Picture (Ferber, Pittman, & Marshall, 2002; The Forum for Youth Investment, 2003d). Children's cabinets and youth coordinating boards or authorities are public sector examples of these coordinating bodies. Community education partnerships and youth futures coalitions are examples of public/private entities (Figure 7.8).

The almost universal challenge with these bodies is how to bring education to the table. The school system, in most cases, exists

- Physical and psychological safety
- Appropriate structure
- Supportive relationships
- Opportunities to belong
- Positive social norms
- Support for efficacy and mattering
- Opportunities for skill building
- Integration of family, school, and community efforts (From the National Research Council & Institute of Medicine, *Community Programs to Promote Youth Development*, 2002)

Figure 7.8   National Research Council's Features of Positive Developmental Settings

as either a dominant or a dormant partner, but rarely as an equal partner. This is a critical shortcoming that must be addressed if community stakeholders are going to have the space and incentives they need to create bolder visions and stronger commitments to ensuring that every child is ready for college, work, and life.

In its 2005 "Call to Action," the National High School Alliance correctly calls for increased youth and community engagement in the high school transformation process (National High School Alliance, 2005). The specific recommendations offered reflect the growing opinion, voiced by Clarence Stone and others, that educators have to see high school reform not "as an administrative or technical puzzle," but a necessary political challenge—"a political challenge not just in the instrumental sense of politics as power, as a way to bring pressure to bear, but also in the broader sense of politics as a process of reorienting the way society operates collectively by changing public institutions and public ideas" (Stone, Henig, Jones, & Pierannunzi, 2001).

We agree and underscore the importance of the word "youth" in the Alliance's call for greater youth and community engagement in the *politics* of high school transformation. We also, however, underscore the importance of youth and community engagement in the *practice* of expanding educational opportunities for high school students and ultimately in showing accountability for both inputs and outcomes.

When the dust settles, it is entirely possible that calls for youth and community engagement will have been met with perfunctory surveys and summits that leave the lion's share of the responsibility for system transformation within the school boundaries. We hope not. But this is likely to be the case unless there is group consensus about the irresponsibility of continuing to promote the idea that educators create a more flexible educational system on their own. Community leaders must be in favor of involving young people, business leaders, higher education institutions, community-based organizations, and other public services providers in the design, implementation, and assessment and delivery of a significantly expanded portfolio of schools.

There is no doubt that improving the life outcomes of America's neediest children and youth will require major improvements in the schools and the community institutions that serve them. The data speak for themselves: young people spend only 25% of their waking hours in school, if they are attending school, and everything the research says about equity and access suggests that young people with weak learning opportunities in school often have weak learning opportunities out of school.

There is no doubt that improving the life outcomes of America's neediest children and youth will require major improvements in the schools and the community institutions that serve them.

There is no doubt that transforming a patchwork of out-of-school programs, however rich, into a real system of out-of-school opportunities will take sustained attention, political leadership, and reprioritized resources. Furthermore, there is increasing certainty among key education reform leaders that completing the job of reforming schools hinges on the rapid buildup of the community-based learning systems:

> If the non-academic system had been organized in a coherent, research-based way, we might not have had to depend upon educators alone for school reform. They would have represented a level of community pressure, because they are closer to the community than schools are. You would have had another equal force at the table. Their questions would have been heard. Part of the reason it has taken so long to get school reform to move is that the pressure has had to come from a handful of well-organized advocates. Imagine if Boys and Girls Clubs and others had said, "we need a system of public education that enables kids to learn and develop." (Wendy Puriefoy, personal communication, December 2001)

The challenge, it seems, is to rally youth advocates and service providers, school reformers, mayors, and others to aggressively blur the lines between systems and time-slots as a deliberate strategy for expanding community commitments to learning writ large, in ways that fully embrace 21st-century demands and opportunities.

We believe that, ultimately, a 21st-century vision of learning and learning supports will have to embrace the possibility that

- young people need a broader range of skills, competencies, and experiences;
- that the education system can and should play the central role in the certification of competence, but that competence does not have to be linked to seat time in the school building; and
- a host of learning organizations can and should be certified and funded to provide requisite learning supports.

Taken together, then—21st-century skills, 21st-century content, and 21st-century contexts for learning—these are the tools communities need to build to ensure that every young person is ready for college, work, and life.

REFERENCES

Afterschool Investments Project. (2005). *State afterschool profiles: Massachusetts*. Washington, DC: The Finance Project and the National Governors Association Center for Best Practices.

America's Promise. (2005). *Voices study: Research findings*. Alexandria, VA: Author.

Baer, J. D., Cook, A. L., & Baldi, S. (2006). *The literacy of America's college students: The National Survey of America's College Students*. Washington, DC: American Institutes for Research.

Bill and Melinda Gates Foundation. (n.d.). *High-quality high schools. Fact sheet*. Seattle, WA: Author.

Blank, M. J., Melaville, A., & Shah, B. P. (2003, May). *Making the difference: Research and practice in community schools*. Washington, DC: The Coalition for Community Schools.

Campaign for Youth. (2005). *Memo on reconnecting our youth*. Washington, DC: Author.

Coalition for Community Schools Web site: www.communityschools.org

Colorado Commission on Higher Education. (2005). *Remedial education: One-third of incoming college students unprepared by K-12 high schools*. Denver: Author.

Council of Chief State School Officers and the Forum for Youth Investment. (2001, April). *Students continually learning: A report of presentations, student voices and state actions*. Washington, DC: The Forum for Youth Investment.

Ferber, T., & Pittman, K., with Marshall, T. (2002). *State youth policy: Helping all youth to grow up fully prepared and fully engaged.* Washington, DC: The Forum for Youth Investment.

The Forum for Youth Investment (2003a, September). Community partnerships for learning: Blurring the lines. *Forum Focus, 1*(2).

The Forum for Youth Investment. (2003b). *Out-of-school-time policy commentary #3: Reflections on system building: Lessons from the after-school movement.* Washington, DC: Author.

The Forum for Youth Investment. (2003c). *Out-of-school-time policy commentary #2: High school after-school: What is it? What might it be? Why is it important?* Washington, DC: Author.

The Forum for Youth Investment. (2003d, November). A portfolio approach to youth policy. *Forum Focus, 1*(3).

The Forum for Youth Investment. (2004a). High school: The next frontier for after-school advocates? *Forum Focus, 2*(1).

The Forum for Youth Investment. (2004b, September). Education pipeline. *Forum Focus, 2*(4).

The Forum for Youth Investment. (2005). *Out-of-school-time policy commentary #10: Rethinking the high school experience: What's after-school got to do with it?* Washington, DC: The Forum for Youth Investment.

Gambone, M. A., Klem, A. M., & Connell, J. P. (2002). *Finding out what matters for youth: Testing key links in a community action framework for youth development.* Philadelphia: Youth Development Strategies, Inc., and Institute for Research and Reform in Education.

Goodlad, J. (1984). *A place called school: Prospects for the future.* New York: McGraw-Hill.

Greene, J. P., & Winters, M. A. (2005). *Public high school graduation and college readiness rates: 1991–2002. Education Working Paper No. 8.* New York: The Manhattan Institute for Policy Research.

High/Scope Educational Research Foundation. (n.d.). *Youth program quality assessment.* Ypsilanti, MI: Author.

Hill, P. T., Campbell, C., & Harvey, J. (2000). *It takes a city: Getting serious about urban school reform.* Washington, DC: Brookings Institution Press.

Jobs for the Future. (2002). *Learning outside the lines: Six innovative programs that reach youth.* Boston: Author.

Joselowsky, F., & Yohalem, N., with Rob Schamberg, R. (2005, May) *District/community alliances to transform high schools: Lessons learned from California's High School Pupil Success Act.* Washington, DC, The Forum for Youth Investment.

Larson, R. (2000). Toward a psychology of positive youth development. *American Psychologist, 55,* 170–183.

National Center for Education Statistics. (2004). Current expenditure per pupil in average daily attendance in public elementary and secondary schools, by state or jurisdiction: Selected years, 1959–60 to 2001–02. *Digest for Education Statistics, 2004.* Washington, DC: Author.

National Governors Association. (2005). *Graduation counts: A report of the National Governors Association Task Force on State High School Graduation Data.* Washington, DC: Author.

National High School Alliance. (2005). *A call to action. Transforming high school for all youth.* Washington, DC: Institute for Educational Leadership.

National Research Council & Institute of Medicine. (2002). *Community programs to promote youth development.* A project of the Board on Children, Youth, and Families, Division of Behavioral and Social Sciences and Education. Washington, DC: National Academy Press.

National Research Council & Institute of Medicine. (2004, November). List of personal and social assets that facilitate positive youth development. In *Community Programs to Promote Youth Development.* Washington, DC: National Academy Press. Report Brief available online at http://www.bocyf.org/youth_development_brief.pdf

Naughton, S., & Teare, C. (2005). The financing of California's after school programs: Preparing for implementation of Proposition 49. Oakland, CA: Children Now.

Partnership for 21st Century Skills. (2003). *Learning for the 21st century: A report and mile guide for 21st century skills.* Washington, DC: Author.

Partnership for 21st Century Skills. (2005). *The assessment of 21st century skills: The current landscape.* Washington, DC: Author.

Pittman, K., & Tolman, J. (2002). *New directions in school reform: Youth-focused strategies versus youth-centered reform.* Washington, DC: The Forum for Youth Investment.

Pittman, K., & Yohalem, N. (2002, April). *Off the shelf and into the field: Making the most of the national research council's new report, Community Programs to Promote Youth Development.* Washington, DC: The Forum for Youth Investment.

Stone, C. N., Henig, J. R., Jones, B. D., & Pierannunzi, C. (2001). *The politics of reforming urban schools.* Lawrence: University of Kansas Press.

Swanson, C. (2004). *Who graduates? Who doesn't? A statistical portrait of public high school graduation, class of 2001.* Washington, DC: The Urban Institute.

Time Warner Foundation. (2003, June). *21st century literacy: A vital component in learning.* Survey conducted by Lake Snell Perry & Associates and Market Strategies. New York: Author.

Tolman, J. (Ed.). (2000). *Learning for life: Youth voices for educational change*. Washington, DC: The Forum for Youth Investment.

U.S. Department of Education. (2003). *No child left behind: transforming America's high schools*. Issue paper from the National High School Summit. Washington, DC: Author.

Yohalem, N., Wilson-Ahlstrom, A., & Yu, D. (2005).*Youth program quality assessment and improvement: Celebrating progress and surfacing challenges. A meeting report*. Washington, DC: The Forum for Youth Investment.

Note: Karen Pittman and Merita Irby cofounded the Forum for Youth Investment in 1998. For more information, visit the Forum's Web site, www.forumfyi.org

CHAPTER EIGHT

COMPASSIONATE INTERVENTION

Helping Failing Schools to Turn Around

ALAN BOYLE

Turning failing schools around is a political imperative. With children's education at stake, and no second chances, there are strong moral reasons to sort things out quickly. While two years may seem a short time in terms of educational change, for a pupil in a failing school, it represents lasting damage to their progress that may never be recovered. So speed is essential, but *real change* is most important. Although Stoll and Myers (1998) contend that there are no quick fixes, I suggest that there are quicker ways to repair failing schools than we have previously found comfortable.

Simply talking tough isn't sufficient, however. Leave that to the politicians. By applying our knowledge of the change process, and with sufficient resources, we can support school recovery in less than two years—and this is about 18 months too long for the sake of the children in the school. By sharing effective ways of intervening in schools, and remembering that there are no guarantees of success, we should learn from each other and maybe hasten the process even further. Early intervention has a double impact: It prevents more serious decline and it speeds up recovery.

Perhaps it is the urgency of repairing such schools and preventing further damage to students' learning that makes compassionate intervention sound inappropriate for a failing school. I understand that, but our experience in working with underperforming schools indicates that compassionate intervention works faster, lasts longer, and costs less in both financial and emotional terms than other types of intervention. If that sounds surprising, then read on.

Working with failing schools carries high risks. If this kind of work excites you, here's a word of caution: Knights in shining armor should not apply. Anyone who thinks he or she can turn around a school from *outside* is deluding him- or herself. Intervention is essential, but it should be thoughtful and compassionate. The only heroes and heroines that emerge from a turnaround school are the staff and students within.

In this chapter, I present the view that

- There is a powerful moral imperative to improve failing schools
- Failing schools can only be fixed from within
- Intervention will accelerate recovery
- No intervention strategy is guaranteed to work in all schools
- Compassionate intervention is efficient and repairs collateral damage
- Compassionate intervention creates better conditions for sustained improvement

Attention was drawn to school failure by a three-year project on "Combating Failure at School" carried out by the Organisation for Economic Co-operation and Development (OECD) between 1994 and 1997. Interest in the United Kingdom was already widespread following the identification of failing schools by a national inspection process launched in 1993. By the end of 2000, about 1,200 schools required "special measures"—the euphemism used in England to describe failing schools. This represented approximately 3% of primary schools, 3% of secondary schools, 8% of special schools, and 6% of pupil referral units (Cribb, 2001, p. 65).

The chaos inherent in failing schools may mean that an intervention strategy that is successful in one school has no effect in another.

Faced with the problem of identified failing schools, Connor Spreng (2005) suggests that government has three possible options:

- Tolerate failing schools
- Change the system of public education
- Devise a strategy of interventions (p. 1)

In 2001, the No Child Left Behind Act (NCLB) rejected the first of these options in the United States by legislating prescribed interventions in response to school failure. Action has not been confined to the United States. However, despite widespread concern and action worldwide, research is limited and little is known about what kinds of interventions are most likely to work (Brady, 2003; Spreng, 2005; Ziebarth, 2002). The chaos inherent in failing schools may mean that an intervention strategy that is successful in one school has no effect in another. At least, that is true of my experience working with failing schools in London, England.

DEFINITION

So, what is a failing school? Let us admit that researchers may never agree on a single definition of failing schools (Connelly, 1999, cited in Spreng, 2005). Nonetheless, practitioners will get on with the repairs that they perceive as necessary. I use the outcomes of schooling to devise a definition of a failing school. If schools are about learning and teaching, then the outcomes of these processes will be pupils' progress in learning. The most reliable indicators for this are the performance of the school's pupils in external tests or examinations, judged against the following:

- The prior attainment of those pupils
- Performance of schools with a similar intake of pupils

In England, we have a national database that tracks the progress of all pupils on national tests at ages 7, 11, 14, and 16. Socioeconomic information is added, based on the postal code of students' home addresses, as well as the schools they attend. We provide schools with detailed and contextualized analyses of their pupils' progress to inform the school's self-evaluation.

A failing school is one in which pupils make very little progress in relation to their prior attainment; consequently, the value-added analyses of the school's test scores are very low when compared with similar schools.

This definition may be extended to include some process indicators. In 1997, for example, the Office for Standards in Education (OFSTED) published a report about the first 200 schools identified as failing in England and Wales. Their conclusion is not particularly revealing, but it does widen the definition.

> There is no doubt that the three most consistent factors found in weak schools are the underachievement of pupils, unsatisfactory or poor teaching and ineffective leadership. (OFSTED, 1997, p. 4)

This description puts the burden of failure on leadership and teachers in the failing school. While school leaders must bear some responsibility when schools fail, this is not always a helpful analysis; it is a spotlight that ignores the shadows around it. Let's explore those shadows a little.

A Moral Imperative

Complexity theory talks about "strange attractors" from which patterns emerge. With failing schools, poverty is one such strange attractor. As the first failing schools were identified in England, and the national failure rate was less than 2%, the government soon realized that there is a common link between socioeconomic deprivation and failing schools. A total of 7% of schools with disadvantaged pupils were found to be failing, compared with the national failure rate of 1.5 to 2% (Department for Education and Employment [DfEE] and OFSTED, 1995, p. 12). By 2005, an estimated 29% of all failing schools were located in the most deprived 20% of communities (National Audit Office, 2006).

> One major reason school failure is a concern is that it tends to disproportionately affect economically disadvantaged children. To say that there is a strong connection between failing schools and the children most in need of good educational opportunities is in part tautology, since the performance of schools is inferred from the analysis of student achievement data. But it also points to a deeper issue that school failure raises. The concern with school failure is almost invariably a concern with the equitable access to public education. (Spreng, 2005, p. 25)

The reality of our inner cities and housing projects that concentrate low-income families in particular neighborhoods cannot be ignored. The interplay of multiple deprivations gives some schools extraordinary challenges (Pattison & Munby, 2001).

Generations of children born in the most deprived parts of urban areas form what Johnson (1999) describes as an "underclass" in our society:

By 2005, an estimated 29% of all failing schools were located in the most deprived 20% of communities.

> Its members are separated from the rest of society by what appears to them to be a permanent inability to sustain themselves economically. The separation creates its own class identity and class culture, which is antagonistic to the rest of society, and to the state. State education is one of the institutions which bears the brunt of this antagonism. . . . Schools for the underclass . . . are defined by their intake. The culture of the underclass dominates these schools . . . the underclass youths look at least as aggressive and threatening to classmates as they do to the staff who try to contain them. (pp. 3–5)

In his shocking book *Failing School, Failing City,* Martin Johnson observes and analyzes the behavior of students in what he describes as schools for the underclass, with high proportions of students from deprived backgrounds. His damning conclusion for government and policy makers points a way forward that will be uncomfortable for some:

> There is considerable correspondence between "underclass school" and "failing school." Dealing with failing schools and failing teachers has become a preoccupation of governments. The employment of slogans and quick-fix initiatives gives the impression of dynamism and progress. However, it is necessary to be rigorous in analysis and honest in policy if the realities are to be addressed. I have not found much of either within the discourse on failing schools. (Johnson, 1999, p. 6)

This is tough talk indeed from a professional who worked for many years in some of the toughest schools in the United Kingdom. For most children born in these circumstances, there are two routes to prosperity: education and crime. If the schools they attend fail to meet their needs, then everyone suffers the consequences. This is the pragmatic imperative.

THE DARK SIDE OF THE MOON

But not all failing schools are located in our most deprived communities. In fact, the differences between individual failing schools are greater than their common characteristics. This is a key consideration when thinking about how best to fix them. I will return to this consideration later in the chapter.

Failing schools are not a new phenomenon. Schools and local authorities (school districts) have dealt with the same issues before (Brady, 2003), but usually without rigorous systems of accountability. Michael Barber explored the controversial topic in his 1995 Greenwich lecture, "The Dark Side of the Moon: Imagining an End to Failure in Urban Education":

> The traditional response to those who raise the question of failure was to suggest that we should discuss the success of the many, not the failure of the few. This is a classic false dichotomy which the debates of the mid-1990s have begun to unmask. A serious debate about failure is, in fact, a precondition of success. "Success for All" and "Zero Tolerance of Failure" turn out to be synonymous. (Barber, 1997, p. 153)

One problem was that we were not discussing and sharing our experiences of dealing with school failure. The literature about turning failing schools around was quite thin in 1993 when we first began to deal with schools that were publicly identified as failing in England. However, we did know that the methods used to improve effective schools were not going to have the same success in failing schools:

> Classical OD (organizational process and problem-oriented approaches) . . . seems to depend on fairly stable environmental conditions, and a certain level of favorable attitude and initial propensity for collective problem solving. Thus this form of OD probably does not represent the most appropriate strategy for change in turbulent urban schools. (Fullan, Miles, & Taylor, 1980, p. 151)

> Our understanding is weakest in relation to schools that are complete failures. In these schools, the processes of school improvement that work in other schools do not succeed. (Barber, 1997, p. 133)

It takes courage and compassion to help turn around schools—tough love, if you will. The precision and skills of a surgeon are required. A blunt approach—too often recommended by policy makers—usually makes things worse, certainly not better, further delaying improvement and causing even longer suffering for the children in the school. Typical of the blunter approach is the public naming and shaming of failing schools. In England and Wales since 1993, inspection reports have been published that label certain schools as failing to provide an acceptable standard of education. Policy makers in the United States have published lists of schools, since 2002, that do not make adequate yearly progress. This brutal approach to school failure may win public approval for politicians, but I wonder, have they even considered the cost of their votes in terms of the damage to people in those schools—most of all those already deprived students for whom there is no escape? They create additional barriers to change just when common sense says we need fewer.

It takes courage and compassion to help turn around failing schools—tough love, if you will. The precision and skills of a surgeon are required.

Barriers to Change

Six years after the naming of failing schools began, OFSTED produced a report identifying the main obstacles that faced failing schools in England. This report is drawn from the observations of Her Majesty's Inspectors (HMI) who had been monitoring the progress of the first 250 failing schools that were turned around. The main barriers to change included the following:

- Anger about the label of "failure," which can take a long time to dissipate
- Weaknesses in the head teacher's, or acting head teacher's, management strategies
- The length of time required to stabilize staffing
- Complacency among some staff, both those new to the school and those who do not recognize they need to alter their practice

- Inconsistencies in managing pupils' behavior
- Insufficient knowledge about how to develop the curriculum
- Difficulties in changing attendance patterns
- Low expectations of pupils' ability to achieve high standards
- Lack of appropriate support from the local authority, governors, trainers, and parents
- An inability to understand what monitoring and evaluation mean, in practice (OFSTED, 1999, p. 2)

Some of these barriers are more easily broken down than others. The most difficult changes to make, and to sustain, are improvements in the quality of pupils' work. Poor work habits, short attention spans, and lack of basic skills accumulate while schools are in a declining state and take some time to reverse and show secure improvement.

David Reynolds (1998) suggests a three-dimensional barrier to change exists, made up of a combination of organizational, cultural, and relational difficulties. Any one of these barriers would be challenging to break, but all three together present a truly formidable obstacle to change. I have analyzed the change barriers identified by HMI and Reynolds according to (1) those associated with willingness to change, and (2) those linked to the capacity for change. I will return to the relationship between capacity and willingness later when I describe a strategy for intervention.

Barriers affected by willingness to change	Barriers affected by capacity for change
Anger about the label "failure"	Weak management skills
Complacency	Unstable staffing
Attendance (by pupils)	Pupils' behavior
Culture (fatalism, pessimism, hostility)	Teachers' curriculum knowledge
Relational patterns (cliques, fractiousness)	Low expectations (teachers and pupils) Monitoring and evaluation Organizational problems

BREAKING BARRIERS

The first thing to tackle is the collateral damage caused by simply being identified as a failing school. Here is a head teacher (principal) of a school who went through the process of recovery and improvement, writing after the events:

> The issue for me was, and still is, how to make those so-called "quick fixes" stick and become embedded in good practice, for what OFSTED inspections do not take account of is what the label "FAILED" does to teachers' morale and self-confidence. ... I believe that unless staff have the self-confidence and professionalism to take on board the areas for improvement, the action plan has no chance of succeeding or of having the desired long-term effect of improving teaching and learning. (Turner, 1998, p. 97)

The shock, depression, and disillusionment associated with being identified with a failing school is generally recognized as widespread (National Audit Office, 2006); the trauma, stress, and declining morale are confirmed by external research (National Foundation for Educational Research [NFER], 1999). Research from inside failing schools (Nicolaidou & Ainscow, 2005) suggests that the experience of being characterized as failing can act as a barrier to the creation of more collaborative ways of working. Unless the collateral damage of being identified as a failing school is first dealt with, chances of any recovery are remote.

In my experiences working with failing schools, counseling techniques are essential for dealing with traumatized staff, who frequently experience grief caused by what they feel is public humiliation. Time is often the greatest healer for this kind of emotional upheaval, but with a failing school there is no time to wait. Compassionate intervention will help.

COMPASSIONATE INTERVENTION

Richard Boyatzis and Annie McKee describe three essential elements of leadership, compassion, hope, and mindfulness, that enable renewal and sustain resonant leadership. They define compassion as empathy and caring in action (Boyatzis & McKee, 2005, p. 178). It goes beyond the common, passive understanding that links compassion with empathy and caring for others in pain, to include a willingness to act on those feelings of care and empathy. They see compassion as the emotional expression of the virtue of benevolence.

For effective intervention in a failing school, you need to care enough to learn from the people in the school. Try to feel what they feel and see the world as they see it—and then do something with what you've learned from them.

I agree that compassion is a highly desirable leadership trait. From my experience in working with failing schools, I would go further to say that it is essential in turnaround strategies. For effective intervention in a failing school, you need to care enough to learn from the people in the school. Try to feel what they feel and see the world as they see it—and then do something with what you've learned from them.

Here Boyatzis and McKee (2005) explain why compassion is crucial for conditions that are familiar in failing schools:

> Conversely, as much as we need to show compassion in order for renewal to take place, we must also receive it. When we are in emotional turmoil and especially when we find that some of our life's foundations are crumbling, we need to know, if we are to repair this situation, that we are not alone. As we are cultivating mindfulness and beginning to feel a glimmer of hope, we also need to know that others care, that they are offering us their concern, compassion and love. We need others' positive regard, even respect, in order to hold on while we figure things out and find ourselves again. (p. 77)

Those are some of the reasons why I have formed a concept of "compassionate intervention" for failing schools. There are two other important reasons to support the concept, as will be described in practice later:

1. It is efficient because it supports more rapid improvement and costs less than other forms of intervention.

2. It is more effective because it provides a better foundation for continued improvement.

Compassionate intervention is essentially *the application of emotional intelligence to leadership in a failing school.* Richard Ackerman and Pat Maslin-Ostrowski (2002) describe how real leadership emerges in times of crisis in their book, *The Wounded Leader.* They conclude that

> One of the gifts of a keen emotional intelligence is the ability to be responsive in practice to the culture of the school so that, in addition to adapting herself to her organisation's culture, the leader is learning to help the culture adapt in ways that allow the culture to flourish for everyone. This kind of leadership requires conscious and skillful development of a supportive environment that learns to manage and adapt to its problems collectively—that is, a culture that truly depends on the knowledge and leadership of the group. Rather than always pointing the finger somewhere else, especially and only toward the leader, the school can be remolded to reflect a culture of shared responsibility for what happens, as well as what does not happen. (p. 131)

By sparking resonance with people in challenging circumstances, you stand a better chance of gaining their commitment to recovery and their willingness to change. Encouraging staff to be more willing to change takes time. For those who are willing, and may have been willing before but were isolated, and those who become more willing, intervention is necessary because the school lacks sufficient capacity. However, the *level* of intervention is critical; it requires careful consideration and precision.

We need to know clearly where we are heading, but remain flexible enough to get there in different ways, preferably by the shortest possible route.

Above all else, we need to know clearly where we are heading, but remain flexible enough to get there in different ways, preferably by the shortest possible route. The improvement of any school is more an organic process than a mechanical one, and consequently it contains an element of unpredictability. For failing schools, the process is even more unpredictable, so our strategy must allow us to be nimble and agile.

Intervention in Inverse Proportion to Success

Education policy in the United Kingdom has used the phrase "intervention in inverse proportion to success" almost as a slogan since 1997. Ronald Brady (2003) analyzed and classified the variety of interventions in failing schools that had been tried out in over 30 jurisdictions across 22 states and the federal government in the United States since 1989. Spreng (2005) later refined Brady's classification, informed by interventions in New Zealand as well as the United States:

Mild Interventions

- Identification—public identification of failing schools
- Planning—requiring a school to prepare a school improvement plan
- Technical assistance—providing advice from an external consultant
- Professional development—providing training for teachers that is linked to the school improvement plan
- Parent involvement—requiring parental involvement in the school
- Tutoring—providing extra classes after school and on weekends
- Change of financing—additional funds to support the improvement plan

Moderate Interventions

- Increasing instructional time—extending the school day
- Audits—inspecting the school with a professional team that publishes a report with recommendations
- Schoolwide action plan—implementation of a comprehensive school reform plan in line with an external audit
- School choice—offering students in failing schools the option of attending another, non-failing, school
- Restriction of autonomy—reducing the principal's authority over the budget, curriculum, and other matters
- Change of principal—replacing the existing principal with a new leader

Strong Interventions

- Reconstitution—replacing all (or almost all) of a school's staff and leadership
- School takeover—handing over governance of a school to either the state or an outside provider
- School closure—closing the school outright

Rather than a complete list of interventions, this was meant to be a list of the most common interventions applied under the jurisdictions of different states. The list concurs with my experience working for a school district in London from 1993 until 2000 (Boyle, 2001).

In England, all schools are audited regularly by teams of external inspectors to inform the school's own improvement plan. Failing schools are identified in the process and then required to produce a comprehensive school reform plan within 40 days. The local authority (school district) is also required to develop its own action plan, within 10 days of the school's own plan, to show how they will intervene and support the school. In managing the interventions in 11 failing schools,

At first, the unpredictability of success baffled us. What worked well in one failing school had no impact in another, similar situation.

and a similar number with serious weaknesses, we used all the interventions listed by Spreng, and more. Not all interventions were used in every school, but different combinations were used with each school.

At first, the unpredictability of success baffled us. What worked well in one failing school had no impact in another, similar situation. This was among the lessons learned by Mintrop and Trujillo (2004) in their evaluation of intervention strategies used in seven states and two large school districts. They observed that

- Sanctions and increasing pressures are not the fallback solution
- No single strategy has been universally successful
- Staging should be handled with flexibility
- A comprehensive bundle of strategies is key
- Relationship-building needs to complement powerful programs
- Competence reduces conflict
- Strong state commitment is needed to create system capacity

These observations reinforce my own experience in England, especially the first point above. It was through the struggle of trying to make sense of our actions that we developed our understanding of compassionate intervention.

A Policy for Compassionate Intervention

Intervention in failing schools in the United Kingdom is first the responsibility of the local authority (school district), with national government watchdogs ready to pounce if things do not work out as desired. By 1998, I was leading a local authority team in London that had five years' experience dealing with failing schools. We were able to draw on this experience to articulate a local policy to support continuous improvement in all schools in our district, which included 12 high schools, 73 elementary schools, and five special schools.

Our policy was developed from tacit knowledge gained by working simultaneously with 11 failing schools and another dozen with serious weaknesses. It was boosted by the collective wisdom of our colleagues in other local school districts around the country whom we invited to join us at a national conference about failing schools in 1997. Our collaboration shared insights between school districts that were supporting failing schools. The conference highlighted what had worked, and what had not worked, to help fix 200 ailing and failing schools. The conference report, "Learning From Failure," provided a framework to articulate our local policy:

> The best policies [for failing schools] are those born out of experience and practice and which recognise the importance of flexibility in applying the policy within an accepted framework in order to make a response to the school's individual circumstances. (OFSTED, 1998, p. 7)

The policy assumed that schools are responsible for their own improvement and that they have effective self-evaluation systems. When a school, or the local school district, first identifies a problem, we then informed the governing body (school board) and requested an action plan to tackle the issue. If there was insufficient progress with a school's action plan after six months, it was time to intervene. At that point, we had to act swiftly and smoothly, but with compassion. The key questions to ask were these:

- What is the school's capacity for improvement?
- How willing is the school to make major changes?

This takes us back to the classification of change barriers listed earlier. Capacity for improvement is a concept built around the school's combined qualities of self-evaluation, leadership, learning, and teaching. In failing schools, this is bound to be low, unless there has been a recent change of leadership within the school. If there is any doubt, capacity for improvement is easily assessed by experienced consultants who visit the school for one or two days, watching lessons and talking with staff and pupils.

Willingness to change relates to the attitudes of staff, governors, and pupils in the face of clear evidence that the school has serious weaknesses. This is trickier to evaluate. I look for *evidence of action rather than intention*. But then how do you distinguish those who may have the greatest will in the world but could not act to save themselves, let alone the school? In the end, it comes down to openness and mutual respect.

To gain respect, I believe you must first give it to others. Respecting other people's views and opinions is not the same as agreeing with them. Working in a failing school, you frequently have to disagree with people in an agreeable manner. Respect is not about deference. Experts going into a failing school to help staff turn the school around should never assume respect for the ideas or contributions they bring to the school. They have to earn it first. There is no inherent debt due to their previous expertise or professional status.

If you go to help a failing school, do not expect expressions of esteem or gratitude—or even a willingness to cooperate. Instead, first show respect for the people in the school and expect to learn from them, no matter how bleak the situation may seem at first. This is the key, not only to the start of the recovery process but also to any chance of sustained improvement beyond recovery. External prescription may give you some quick wins; however, without respect for the views, ideas, and experience of those in the school—and the construction of the school's capacity from that baseline—you will never get beyond recovery and "over the rainbow." I return to this point later.

If you go to help a failing school, do not expect expressions of esteem or gratitude—or even a willingness to cooperate. Instead, first show respect for the people in the school and expect to learn from them, no matter how bleak the situation may seem at first.

Sara Lawrence-Lightfoot (2000) lays out six dimensions of respect. They are touchstones for compassionate intervention:

- Empowerment—intervention should be to enable the school to improve itself
- Healing—it is through your healing actions that you will exhibit and develop compassion

- Dialogue—learning how to ask good questions and listen to others
- Curiosity—endless inquiry, creating relationships, and engaging in conversations
- Self-respect—avoiding deference and helping others to value themselves
- Attention—giving your undiluted attention by listening to what the school wants (pp. 11–13)

Returning to the strategy, our assessments of capacity and willingness determined our level of intervention. We didn't always get it right the first time, but the flexibility of our policy enabled us to shift between intervention levels with agility. There is a clear distinction between intervention and interference. Intervention provides

- A working partnership that shares responsibility for the problem and ownership of the solution
- Intensive support and advice for managers, and in the classroom, this is linked to an action plan
- Determined action to improve or remove ineffective teachers or managers

Interference, on the other hand, is perceived when the level of intervention is inappropriate to the situation in the school. This is discussed later under the "False Start" subsection.

The different levels of external intervention in failing schools and those with serious weaknesses are illustrated in the following chart, based on the responses to the two questions mentioned above. This is our interpretation of the phrase "intervention in inverse proportion to success." If you use this strategy, consider the level of intervention carefully and then explain to the school how, and why, you will intervene. Better still, when schools understand the strategy, they are able to suggest the appropriate level of intervention.

I have described how we used this strategy and the different actions associated with each quadrant in Figure 8.1 elsewhere (Boyle, 2001, 2004). The trajectory for a school with low capacity that was unwilling to change would be to intervene and takeover for up to 6 months, empower the school through coaching over the next 12 months, and continue with light touch stimulation for up to a further 6 months. Turnaround should happen in less than two years.

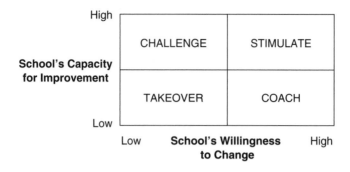

Figure 8.1   Intervention Strategy in Schools Causing Serious Concern

There is some overlap among three of these four positions with Brady's and Spreng's classifications of interventions: mild (stimulate), moderate (coach), and strong (takeover). Although we used a wider range of takeover options than those listed by Spreng, it is the fourth quadrant—in which schools have capacity but no willingness for change—that is most different.

CHALLENGE

Schools that are unwilling to change despite having the capacity to do so are sometimes called "coasting" schools; their staff members are complacent about the situation. Test scores appear reasonable because the school has a more privileged population of pupils. But careful analysis of the progress made by students based on their prior attainment shows that the school is actually failing. Such schools present the greatest challenge of all to change. That challenge needs to be turned back onto the school itself.

An objective analysis of data should provide a starting point for discussion with the principal. However, the principal must also be listened to—and with respect. The principal's views and reasons for opposition need to be carefully explored, but challenged with compassion. Support to help staff analyze the school's performance data should be offered in case they lack that specific capacity. Targets for improving standards and the quality of education that are in line with targets set by other similar schools should be discussed. How the school might achieve those targets is up to them, but as long as there is an ongoing dialogue about their ways of working, then it may be possible to develop a creative response that will allow progress.

Trust is essential for all concerned in order to find the common ground on which to build a future that takes the school out of failure. But there have to be limits to how long failure can be tolerated.

Working with such a school requires patience and integrity. Intervention may be carried out by an independent negotiator who has earned the respect of both the school and the local authority. Trust is essential for all concerned in order to find the common ground on which to build a future that takes the school out of failure.

But there have to be limits to how long failure can be tolerated. My rule of thumb would be six months, about the same length of time spent in "takeover," as described above.

What if the school still won't change after six months? Then the principal's capability requires greater scrutiny, and appropriate procedures should be applied. As with teachers that are not up to scratch, there can be no slip-up regarding the agreed-upon procedure. At first it may seem that the process will never end, but with compassion, determination, and creativity, the problems are usually sorted more quickly than expected once official procedures are instigated. If not, you will need to shift into "takeover" mode and go on from there.

Fresh Start

The uncertainties associated with failing schools require that serious consideration be given to closing the school. Anyone who has ever tried to close a school will know the kind of opposition that will be faced. It reminds me of a comment I once heard, that change is like moving a graveyard: you never know how many friends the dead have until you try to move them. Closing a school is much the same.

Sometimes complete closure of the school is not an option because there is such a high demand for an operating school in the area. The UK government introduced the "Fresh Start" program in 1997 as a means of replacing schools suffering long-term poor performance and schools with which other options had failed. The school is closed and a new school is opened on the same site, with the same students, but with a new name, and a different staff, ethos, and curriculum. In the United States, some states use a similar process called "reconstitution."

There have been 51 Fresh Start schools in the United Kingdom (23 primary, 27 secondary, and one special school) since the program was launched. It has not yet been formally evaluated, but analysis of performances on public exams in the 27 secondary schools suggests that, on average, they are performing better than their predecessor schools (National Audit Office, 2006, p. 44). Unfortunately, that's not saying much, since they were so bad before. On average, Fresh Start schools have received £1.6 million each for capital works and £0.6 million extra revenue funding each year over three years. Although the National Audit Office did not assess their cost-effectiveness, they do acknowledge that the Fresh Start program is achieving improved attainment levels for pupils at challenging schools.

False Start

Choosing an inappropriate level of intervention gives a false start to the recovery process. We learned this from painful experience, and more than once. So here are the different kinds of responses that might be experienced by using an inappropriate level of intervention. Under each heading, for the most appropriate kind of intervention, I have listed typical responses to each of the less appropriate strategies.

Takeover (School is unwilling and unable to change)

- Coach—this might eventually catch on, but time and effort will be wasted if the willingness to change is not dealt with urgently. Improvement will be delayed.
- Challenge—this will work, but it wastes six months when something could be done within the school.
- Stimulate—a complete waste of time that will have no real impact as the school is not capable enough to be able to respond.

Coach (School is willing but unable to change)

- Takeover—risky as it could cause resentment and become counterproductive. If the school is willing to change, taking it over may create antagonism so that they become unwilling to cooperate.

- Challenge—because support is not being provided, the school will become frustrated and disillusioned because it doesn't have the capacity to respond. It will reinforce feelings of hopelessness and despair.
- Stimulate—may produce some slow change but without intensive, school-based support, the staff will not develop the skills quickly enough to make significant improvements.

Stimulate (School is willing and able to change)

- Takeover—in this situation, it would be perceived as interference. Apart from being inefficient in terms of the resources available for intervention, it will demoralize and de-skill staff who can improve the school themselves.
- Coach—will probably continue to improve the school but leads to a growing dependency on external support. It will restrict the development of the internal capability of the school.
- Challenge—will probably be ignored and the school may turn elsewhere for the support it still needs. If other sources of support are not available, the fragile school may slide back and improvements will not be sustained.

Challenge (School is unwilling but able to change)

- Takeover—is unlikely to achieve anything. If the school has the capacity to improve, it will use all its ability to frustrate and even sabotage any changes you try to make by taking it over, unless you have a massive clear-out (Fresh Start). Although it may have moral justification, this remains interference.
- Coach—apart from wasting precious resources, the school will consider this approach to be patronizing and their responses may reduce the morale of the change agents. The only thing this brick wall will give you is a headache.
- Stimulate—is probably the next-best option in this circumstance, as long as it is accompanied by prayer. Something has got to shift in the attitude of the school before it will have any real impact.

OVER THE RAINBOW

Judy Garland's poignant song in *The Wizard of Oz* could be an anthem for those working in failing schools: "Birds fly over the rainbow, Why then, oh why can't I?" (Harburg, 1939). The danger is in confusing recovery from failure with being over the rainbow. It definitely is not; there is still a long way to go before the school can be described as good, let alone great.

The cost of recovery in failing schools is high in both emotional and economic terms (National Audit Office, 2006). By recovery, we mean they have shown themselves to be at least satisfactory. After this investment, it is important that the schools should continue to improve. In England, nearly 60%

The cost of recovery in failing schools is high in both emotional and economic terms.

of failing schools were rated "good" or better when they were inspected two years later. Only 5% were assessed as unsatisfactory (National Audit Office, 2006, p. 49). There is still room for improvement, yes, but how?

How you move beyond recovery depends on how you got there. Hargreaves and Fink (2006) analyzed leadership succession around the appointment of principals in terms of whether it was planned or unplanned and whether the intention was to develop continuity or discontinuity. This creates four possibilities: planned continuity, unplanned continuity, planned discontinuity, and unplanned discontinuity (Hargreaves & Fink, 2006, p. 62). Rather than a change of principal, what we are considering here are changes in situation. The school has made the initial change: from failure to recovery. We are now considering moving over the rainbow, from adequate to outstanding.

If the intervention strategy relied heavily on prescription, then continued improvement beyond recovery is unlikely. There is powerful evidence for this in England following the imposed national literacy and numeracy strategies. Prescription across 20,000 primary (elementary) schools saw test results for 11-year-olds shoot up from 1997 to 2000, and then level off for the next four years. Fullan, Hill, and Crévola (2006) describe what they call the "prescription trap" as being seductive because it offers useful start-up results but is ultimately the wrong track.

In order to make the next "breakthrough" (the title of their book), what is needed is precision, not prescription. Therefore, if prescription was your chosen route from failure to recovery, you are likely to need some planned discontinuity in order to get over the rainbow. This is a perverse situation to be in, because by intervening with prescription you were initially exercising planned discontinuity. Successive discontinuity and continuous improvement are mutually exclusive in philosophy. Thirty years of research show that planned discontinuity has been good at shaking things up but not at making changes stick (Hargreaves & Fink, 2006).

Michael Fullan (in press) summarizes the situation:

> When all is said and done, *Turnaround Leadership* is about getting off the road to perdition, and on the road to precision. The road to precision is not one of prescription. It is a matter of being best equipped with capacities that increase the chances of being dynamically precise in the face of problems that are unpredictable in their timing and nature, largely because they arise from human motivation and interaction. (p. 2)

By using compassionate intervention, as outlined in this chapter, I argue that you will not only support more rapid recovery in a school, you will *nurture continued growth*. Giving people respect is not about being nice—it is essential if you hope to develop their self-esteem. Compassionate intervention is not about creating good feelings to mask poor performance. It is about empowering people and restoring or developing their confidence so that they improve their school from within. If encouraging self-reliance and developing capacity for improvement was your route from failure to recovery, then you stand a better chance of flying over the rainbow.

Compassionate intervention is not about creating good feelings to mask poor performance. It is about empowering people and restoring or developing their confidence so that they improve their school from within.

PREVENTION RATHER THAN CURE

If the cost of fixing failing schools seems high (Education Commission of the States [ECS], 2002), the cost of *not* repairing them is even higher. Our experience suggests that timetables for recovery can be cut to less than two years through the application of a flexible and coherent strategy in a compassionate manner. But even that length of time causes lasting damage to the education of those students who are so unfortunate as to attend the school at the time. So, as politicians in England legislate for turning failing schools around in under 12 months (Department for Education and Skills [DfES], 2005), I wonder where it will end.

I believe that we need a culture shift, to move away from fixing problems in ever shorter periods of time, and to find ways of getting it right the first time. One of the remarkably few common features of all failing schools is *isolation.* These schools may have detached themselves from those around them. Possibly they couldn't keep up with the pace of continuous reform that has sometimes been justifiably imposed on schools in recent years. There are many reasons to explain why some schools slip out of the mainstream of professional development.

If the cost of fixing failing schools seems high, the cost of not repairing them is even higher.

Here I turn to Michael Fullan (2005) for the tri-level solution as a more hopeful way forward: "This solution represents a total system focus—a self-conscious attempt at all levels to use the best knowledge to strategize and bring about improvements and build capacity" (p. 210). This kind of change is not about seeking alignment, but rather about making connections and exerting mutual influence.

- At the school level—we have never found a failing school with an effective professional learning community; it's an oxymoron. You should begin to develop an authentic professional learning community through compassionate intervention. Without compassion, you'd be more than lucky to achieve it.

- At the district level—if no school was left behind, there would be no isolated schools, decreasing the likelihood of failing schools. Fullan observes that successful school districts support powerful lateral capacity building between schools. There is a collective moral purpose where principals share districtwide goals and are almost as concerned about the performance of the school down the road as they are about their own school. Collaboration is especially important for high schools.

- At the state level—the most difficult to work with because of the political context. Fullan notes the political proclivity for accountability but argues that accountability without capacity building amounts to little, if any, gain. So to avoid failing schools, rather than deal with their consequences, policy makers should refocus resources to support capacity building as a fundamental characteristic of the system.

As long as we have failing schools, I contend that compassionate intervention, as I have described it, is a more efficient way to repair them. It is more efficient because it costs less in financial terms than "reconstitution" or a "fresh start," and it works faster to build productive professional relationships in the schools. Compassionate intervention should not add to the emotional turmoil caused through the identification of a failing school; it should begin to repair that collateral damage. Compassionate intervention creates resonance so that it actually leads to renewal—not only of the failing school but also those who are providing the compassionate intervention. By decreasing their chronic stress, they renew themselves in mind, body, heart, and spirit.

REFERENCES

Ackerman, R., & Maslin-Ostrowski, P. (2002). *The wounded leader.* San Francisco: Jossey-Bass.

Barber, M. (1997). *The learning game.* London: Indigo.

Boyatzis, R., & McKee, A. (2005). *Resonant leadership.* Boston: Harvard Business School Press.

Boyle, A. (2001). *Turning failing schools around: Intervention in inverse proportion to success.* London: Leannta Education Associates.

Boyle, A. (2004). Faith, hope, and intervention. In A. Blankstein (Ed.), *Failure is NOT an option.* Thousand Oaks, CA: Corwin Press.

Brady, R. (2003). *Can failing schools be fixed?* Washington, DC: Thomas B. Fordham Foundation.

Cribb, M. (2001). Dealing with schools causing concern. In D. Woods & M. Cribb (Eds.), *Effective LEAs and school improvement.* London: Routledge Falmer.

Department for Education and Employment and Office for Standards in Education. (1995). *The improvement of failing schools: UK policy and practice 1993–1995.* London: Author.

Department for Education and Skills. (2005). *Higher standards, better schools for all.* London: Author.

Education Commission of the States. (2002). *State intervention in low-performing schools and school districts.* Denver, CO: Author.

Fullan, M. (2005). Professional learning communities writ large. In R. DuFour, R. DuFour, & R. Eaker (Eds.), *On common ground: The power of professional learning communities.* Bloomington, IN: Solution Tree.

Fullan, M. (in press). *Turnaround leadership.* San Francisco: Jossey-Bass.

Fullan, M., Hill, P., & Crévola, C. (2006). *Breakthrough.* Thousand Oaks, CA: Corwin Press; Toronto: Ontario Principals' Council.

Fullan, M., Miles, M. B., & Taylor, G. (1980). Organizational development in schools: The state of the art. *Review of Educational Research, 50*(1), 212–83.

Harburg, E. Y. (1939). "Over the Rainbow" song in the motion picture *The Wizard of Oz.* Santa Monica, CA: Metro-Goldwyn-Mayer.

Hargreaves, A., & Fink, D. (2006). *Sustainable leadership.* San Francisco: Jossey-Bass.

Johnson, M. (1999). *Failing school, failing city.* Concord, MA: Paul & Co.

Lawrence-Lightfoot, S. (2000). *Respect.* Cambridge, MA: Perseus.

Mintrop, H., & Trujillo, T. (2004). *Corrective action in low-performing schools: Lessons for NCLB implementation from state and district strategies in first-generation accountability systems.* Los Angeles: National Center for Research on Evaluation, Standards, and Student Testing.

National Audit Office. (2006). *Improving poorly performing schools in England.* London: The Stationery Office.

National Foundation for Educational Research. (1999). *The impact of OFSTED inspections.* London: Author.

Nicolaidou, M., & Ainscow, M. (2005). Understanding failing schools: perspectives from the inside. *School Effectiveness and School Improvement, 16*(3), 229–248.

Office for Standards in Education. (1997). *From failure to success.* London: Author.

Office for Standards in Education. (1998). *Making headway.* London: Author.

Office for Standards in Education. (1999). *Lessons learned from special measures.* London: Author.

Pattison, M., & Munby, S. (2001). School improvement partnerships. In D. Woods & M. Cribb (Eds.), *Effective LEAs and school improvement.* London: Routledge Falmer.

Reynolds, D. (1998). The study and remediation of ineffective schools: Some further reflections. In M. Stoll & K. Myers (Eds.), *No quick fixes.* London: Falmer.

Spreng, C. (2005). *Policy options for interventions in failing schools.* Santa Monica, CA: Rand.

Stoll, L., & Myers, K. (1998). No quick fixes: An introduction. In M. Stoll & K. Myers (Eds.), *No quick fixes.* London: Falmer.

Turner, L. (1998). Turning around a struggling school: A case study. In M. Stoll & K. Myers (Eds.), *No quick fixes.* London: Falmer.

Ziebarth, T. (2002). *State takeovers and reconstitutions.* Denver, CO: Education Commission of the States.

CHAPTER NINE

THE CASE
FOR FAILURE

Risk, Innovation, and Engagement

RICHARD FARSON

The problem we face in today's education is not too much failure, but too little. We need much more failure, at all levels: more failing students, failing teachers, failing administrators. We need to fail sooner, faster, and bigger.

One frequent criticism of education is that it has not fundamentally changed in several centuries. Critics of other professions often say that if you're doing what you were trained to do, you're obsolete. Regrettably, that criticism does not seem to apply to teaching.

Education has withstood almost every effort to bring about radical change. Even technology, which has changed almost every other profession, has yet to change elementary and secondary schooling. The inventions that many thought would transform education have essentially come and gone— or, more accurately, been subsumed

Education has withstood almost every effort to bring about radical change.

into the traditional forms of education. The "magic lantern" slide projector, radio, film, television, video, computers—none has had the impact it was expected to have. Like the history of fighting wars with China, where the invading victors were simply absorbed by that giant culture, a parade of educational reformers have sought to bring about fundamental change, only to discover that their successes faded while the existing system remained intact.

That resistance to change might be considered a strength if we could believe that the traditional format has survived these powerful technological interventions because it is such a fundamentally sound system—so reliably effective, so demonstrably rewarding to students, teachers, and society. But with high dropout rates, massive functional illiteracy among graduates, colleges having to offer remedial education to their carefully selected freshmen, Ivy League seniors unable to pass the equivalent of a seventh-grade history exam, most high school students failing exams a few weeks after passing them, our students falling far behind those of other countries in practically every field, half of all teachers leaving the field after less than five years in what many thought would be a career profession—it's hard to say it's working all that well.

MANAGING INNOVATION

If it's already not working well, why add more failure? Not failure for its own sake, obviously. The important reason is this: *Failure is necessary for innovation.* Innovation always requires risk taking, and risk always involves failure. The great innovators failed many times before succeeding.

We can learn much from Charles Kettering, who was second only to Thomas Edison as America's leading inventor, responsible for the automotive self-starter, refrigerants, diesel engines, home air conditioners—more than 200 patents. He thought that genuine innovators were hobbled more than helped by what they learned in school, and that students subjected to the prospect of failing exams and "flunking out" learned a bad lesson: that failure is terminal. A good research man, he would say, failed every time but the last one. If he failed 999 times before finally succeeding, it was only the last one that mattered.

The most successful entrepreneurs have failed at least once. One of them, David Levy, said that when he was working for Apple Computers, his boss told him he wasn't failing enough, and that from now on he wanted to see an 80% failure rate. Thomas Watson, founder of IBM, said, "The fastest way to success is to double your failure rate." Author and filmmaker Michael Crichton says, "If you don't fail a certain percentage of the time, it means you're playing it too safe." Athletes certainly know this. If the tennis player doesn't serve some double faults, or if the skier never falls, it means they are not taking the necessary risks to perform at their very best.

Piggy Lambert, the legendary Purdue University basketball coach, once told his player John Wooden (who eventually became a legendary coach himself), "Remember, the team that makes the most mistakes is going to win." He meant, of course, that they were going try harder, risk tactics and strategies, take more shots. Wooden never forgot that lesson, and employed it with his 10 national championship teams at UCLA.

If we are to bring about educational change, we will certainly have to become less averse to risk and more tolerant of failure. We have been going through a series of management fads beginning with Quality Circles and Total Quality Management and moving on to Zero Defects and Six Sigmas, all driving toward performance close to perfection. But innovation involves trial and error, and is riddled with mistakes and wrong turns. How those experiences are handled by management determines just how innovative the organization can become.

The corporate giant 3M attributes much of its success to its acceptance, even encouragement, of failure. Its most famous example is Post-it notes, which were the product of a failed adhesive, too weak for the work for which it was intended, but later seen as perfect for the concept of semi-adhesive notes. Think of the cultural change that could happen in education if the 3M attitude of encouraging failure was adopted. It may be difficult to imagine a school system embracing that attitude, to picture a superintendent taking a genuine, nonjudgmental interest in the failure of some principal's idea for improvement. But that attitude is strong in the history of innovation, and is spreading in business and industry. We can take a lesson from the Wright Brothers. They were as excited about their failures as they were about their successes.

Making the necessary changes in education will require a special courage—the courage to abandon a program that seems to be working for something that might work better.

Management theorist Warren Bennis interviewed dozens of CEOs to determine what made them successful, and found that their attitude toward failure was often a key. He quotes one of them as saying, "If I have an art form of leadership, it is to make as many mistakes as quickly as I can in order to learn."

Making the necessary changes in education will require a special courage—the courage to abandon a program that seems to be working for something that might work better. That is how our most successful companies are operating. As social theorist Marshall McLuhan famously said, "If it's working, it's obsolete." So the saying, "If it ain't broke, don't fix it" must become, "If it ain't broke, fix it anyway."

MORE FAILING STUDENTS?

The need for failure, for risk taking, for well-intended mistakes, runs deeper than just management concerns, penetrating the learning process itself and affecting every student. Punishing or penalizing failure guarantees that the learning process will never be as experimental, creative, and risky as it needs to be.

The kind of learning that we care most about, the kind that leads to literacy, understanding, awareness, discovery, and personal growth—to wisdom, if you will—is inherently threatening. True education always poses that special kind of threat, arising from the entirely realistic fear that after this learning experience, one's life will not be the same. It can happen in the earliest years and is a genuine threat, requiring courage and risk. That level of learning is not common in today's education because it can only take place in an atmosphere of acceptance and safety, inspired by a motivated and knowledgeable teacher and pursued with the freedom of self-direction. It will always involve many mistakes and failures. Our current educational designs do not often permit such explorations.

The concepts of success and failure are so much a part of schooling, it is difficult to imagine what it might be like without them, but these terms should be dropped from the lexicon of educators. Their disappearance would affect everything we do as students, teachers, and administrators—and, I believe, very much for the better. Neither concept serves us well, nor is either experienced in the way most believe it is. Both are the enemies of intellectual development. Because they were introduced to serve purposes having little to do with learning, they do not belong in the repertory of educators' responses. Children who, after many failed tries, experience the thrill of writing their own names for the first time, or spelling a long word, do not need gold stars.

As you look back over your life, you will discover that success and failure are sometimes indistinguishable, and highly interdependent. I had an occasion to do just that when I attended one of my college reunions. To prepare for it, everyone in our class was asked to submit a paragraph describing what had happened to us since graduation. I first composed a paragraph touching on some of the predictable points: family, homes, jobs, achievements. When I finished, however, I thought it read too much like a resume. Why would I write to my old classmates with such self-serving half-truths? So instead (mainly for my own amusement because I knew the college wouldn't use it), I decided to write my experience the way it really happened. What resulted were several pages full of descriptions of failures, leading to successes, leading to failures, continuing right up to the present. I was struck by how necessary the failures were to my development. Often it was difficult to say which was which, because what seemed a failure or success at one point became the opposite later. I'm sure that if we were completely honest, we would each have such a story to tell.

As basketball star Michael Jordan says, "I've missed more than 9,000 shots in my career. I've lost about 300 games. Twenty-six times I've been trusted to take the winning shot, and missed. I've failed over and over. That's why I succeed."

SEPARATING EDUCATION FROM EVALUATION

The issue, of course, is the pernicious role of *evaluation*. That is what defines our failures, essentially criminalizing them. It is entrenched in all of education, and with the growth of concern over accountability, it becomes even more prominent, and more inhibiting. Ambrose Bierce, writing his *Devil's Dictionary* a century ago, defined accountability as "the mother of caution."

Evaluation has come to dominate school programs, both formally and informally, its putative importance taken for granted by both students and educators. Every

Evaluation has come to dominate school programs, both formally and informally, its importance taken for granted by both students and educators.

aspect of student activity is evaluated, and much of it is graded and reported. Any question answered by a student is typically met with some evaluative comment such as "Good" or "Right." Even classroom behavior ("citizenship") is graded. In short, every move a student makes, academically or socially, is subject to evaluation.

Many, perhaps most, of the reasons for evaluation are not pedagogical, but stem from the management requirements of the school system, and even more from the larger system in which it is embedded. But some of it comes from the belief that there exist certain basic skills and information that students must acquire, and it is for the benefit of the student as well as for the larger system requirements that this acquisition be verified by evaluation.

This belief is founded on the premise that all students should become alike in certain ways, i.e., learn the same skills and information to meet established standards. As long as we view education in this way, it makes perfect sense for us to measure their progress toward that goal. Evaluation helps the teacher diagnose the student's needs, and provides feedback to the student.

But we make no distinction between basic skills and other kinds of learning—all is subject to evaluation and grading. Our ability to measure achievement in learning basic skills has led to our extending that idea of measurement to the full range of learning. Our evaluative posture toward learning Shakespeare is essentially the same as that toward learning to add a column of numbers.

We pay a terrible, but largely invisible, price for indulging in that measurement approach to education. Think about it: Ultimately, do we want our graduates to be alike? No. We want them to be different from each other. That's what education is all about.

Education is the marriage of a person's experience to important concepts. That marriage, that special integration of ideas with experience, forms a unique individual, unlike anyone else. Each student brings to the learning situation a large mass of previously assimilated experience and understanding that shapes whatever the student sees and does, and therefore whatever he or she learns. In educating students, we do not want them to be like everyone else, but to become whatever their own potential might be. We want to individualize them as much as possible. It is in our interest as a society for them to become different from everyone else.

While teaching basic skills, what we usually call training, is directed toward making people alike, true education makes them different. Standardized testing therefore can apply only to training. We cannot assess individual development by applying standards to students we want to be different from each other. But where do we draw the line? At what point does training become education? Teachers are faced with a dilemma. How can they tell when to shift from the evaluative posture that seems efficacious when teaching skills to the non-evaluative posture required for education, where evaluation clearly becomes the enemy of learning? And what system would permit such a shift?

I'm afraid we may not be able to draw that line, and if we seriously think about it, we may decide it is unwise to treat any learning situation evaluatively, even the learning of basic skills. Though we would be tempted to employ such measurement to assessing performance in basic skills, we may not be seeing skill development in all of its potential richness. In evaluating it, we might be limiting the independent growth of our students, just as we are in what seem to be the more advanced areas of learning, such as literature, social studies, history, and so forth. Maybe we do not want everyone to develop skills in the same way.

NO PURE SKILLS

Clearly, there are skills that can be learned—perhaps *must* be learned—and we can test to see if students do indeed learn them. But paradoxically, that statement, like most significant statements, is both true and false, and it may not be true at the most important levels of learning. It may be that in every situation that involves skill, there is also an educational component adding the kind of complexity that makes people different from each other, and therefore beyond the realm of standards and evaluation.

Let's take a few examples. I first thought that learning a language was clearly a testable skill. Presumably, we want students to learn how to pronounce the words exactly the way native speakers do. The more sophisticated and experienced language teachers, however, do not just teach the language as a skill; they teach the culture in which the language is embedded. The reason is that without understanding the subtleties and nuances of culture, we cannot understand the true meaning of the communication. Unless we understand that the word *mañana* (formal definition: tomorrow morning) used by a native Spanish speaker may not mean tomorrow morning at all, but something more like "someday soon" or "later" or "eventually" or maybe "never," we could be greatly misled. Similarly, negotiating with a Japanese businessman who seems to say "Yes" to one of our requests, and not realizing he may actually mean "No" but is culturally prevented from using that term in a friendly discussion, we could get into big trouble.

We pay a terrible, but largely invisible, price for indulging in that measurement approach to education.

We pay a terrible, but largely invisible, price for indulging in that measurement approach to education. Staying with the language example, at the higher levels of language usage, we would not want people to speak or write exactly alike, any more than we would want William Faulkner, James Joyce, Emily Dickinson, Tom Wolfe, Hunter Thompson, and William Shakespeare to sound alike. We can even come to appreciate the different language inventions in which words sometimes take on meanings that are precisely the opposite of their conventional definitions. As I have learned from my skateboarding sons, not only does the term "bad" sometimes mean "good," but the term "sick" can mean "great." So language is only testable at the simplest, and perhaps least interesting, levels. Testing and grading at that level sends what some would regard as a rather limiting message about the use of language.

How about learning an athletic skill—say, learning to serve in tennis? Surely that is a skill that can be learned from a teacher or coach. The best players seem to all do it the same way. But wait a minute—they *don't* do it the same way. Each develops a slightly different serve to accommodate his or her physical abilities, the racquet the player uses, or his or her style of play. Moreover, each time the player serves in a match the serve is further differentiated, informed by an educated response to the situation, a spontaneous reading of the opponent's ability, position on the court, strategy, mood, state of exhaustion, weakness, spirit, momentum or lack of it—and on and on, including any number of other dimensions unconsciously called into play at that moment, determining not just where to place the ball in the serving court, but what kind of speed or spin to put on it, or what to communicate by it. Many of these aspects of the serve are invented by the player, not the coach. So can we test the skill? Yes, but not in its most important dimensions, its finer points. In the end, it's all about the finer points. For a pro, it is learned as education, not skill. I'm sure the same subtleties, complexities, and individual differences apply to quarterbacking, boxing, pitching, or auto racing.

Acting is also considered a skill and usually taught that way—and it surely is a skill. One only need watch the film *The French*

Lieutenant's Woman, where Meryl Streep plays a scene without acting and then replays it employing acting skills, for the viewer to appreciate the power of that skilled craft. Yet no acting coach would settle for just a skilled actor, wanting instead for the actor to merge personal experience and deep feeling into the scripted role and display a broad understanding of the period in history, the writer's intention, the social and cultural context of the drama, the dynamics of the relationships, the nature of playwriting, and so on, all the while inventing and going beyond previous limits on performance, and beyond the coach. Is that skill training or education? Is it testable? Impossible.

I am continually impressed by the attitude of many young rock musicians who take pride in not knowing, and never intending to learn, how to read music. They estimate that half of all rock musicians, including those at the top, do not read music. They have a case, too. Famous stars like pianist Erroll Garner, drummer Buddy Rich, and guitarists Wes Montgomery and Jimi Hendrix never learned to read music. Trumpet idol Chet Baker did not understand the chord structure of music. Famed pianist Dave Brubeck actually graduated from college as a music major without that ability. Legendary jazz trumpeter Louis Armstrong, when questioned as to whether he could read music, answered, "Not enough to hurt my playing." Even the great classical tenor Luciano Pavarotti cannot read music. The list of top musicians without such skills is long, but it is significant to note for this discussion that many stars sought to learn music-reading skills only after becoming accomplished professionals.

What about reading? Surely that is a skill—learning the alphabet, recognizing words, pronouncing the syllables. We can test for accuracy, speed, and comprehension. New methods for teaching the skill are frequently introduced. But we face a curious phenomenon. For most students, the more they are made to acquire the skill, the less they desire to read. As a consequence, after 13 years of full-time study, of the 71% who still remain in school to graduate, it is nothing short of astounding that about half are functionally illiterate. The average high school graduate has not read a book in the last year. It is not much of an exaggeration to say that in school, students learn *not* to read.

The average high school graduate has not read a book in the last year. It is not much of an exaggeration to say that in school, students learn not to read.

Some hold that reading is a skill that, under optimal conditions, takes only a few weeks to learn. What's going on here? I suggest that we are approaching the subject of reading as a skill-training exercise, when it is really a matter for broader education. Measurement of the skill may only get in the way. The larger interests and potential of the individual student should be looked to before any emphasis is placed on skill development. In a sense, we may have had it backwards all along. Perhaps skills are not basic after all. Learning skills does not necessarily lead to more advanced interests, but more advanced interests may lead to learning skills.

We can make a similar case for writing, mathematics, computer skills, drawing, and so forth, perhaps showing that there really is no subject that is purely a matter of skill development. Perhaps it is all education, and for that reason perhaps evaluation is everywhere inappropriate.

That would not be a surprise to many human resources professionals in industry, where they find that evaluative performance reviews are not only dreaded by both the giver and the receiver, but are completely uncorrelated with improvement in productivity. They continue to be used, partly to protect against liability for wrongful termination, and because it is sometimes the only way that upper management can make sure that supervisors will spend any time at all during the year with each of their employees individually.

FURTHER COMPLICATIONS OF EVALUATION

The practice of evaluation raises other questions. For example, we not only want our students to be different from each other, but different from their teachers. What? Don't we want them to learn what the teacher has to teach? Well, yes, but not exactly. Ideally, we want the student to transcend the teacher, to go further with some ideas and to creatively set a different course. How can we possibly measure that, or even know that it is happening?

Indeed, we know from history that such paradigm-changing ideas are first met with ridicule, then hatred, then grudging acceptance. We don't need to go back to Freud or Darwin or Galileo to find those reactions. When Frederick Smith, as a student, submitted his business plan for Federal Express, his professor handed it back with a C grade, advising him that he needed to present something realistic. I am similarly amused, as well as disturbed, that Maya Lin received a B for her design of the Vietnam Veterans' Memorial. Both of these evaluative sins were committed at Yale, one of our top institutions of learning. Think what goes on in our lesser institutions. In its upper reaches, certainly, educational achievement is totally beyond conventional evaluation.

Evaluating education is complicated by other factors as well. Take timing, for example. Evaluations are typically administered right after a lesson is delivered, or at the end of the week, or end of the semester. But when is a lesson learned? A lesson may have been highly effective, but the effect may be dormant for years. I still occasionally find myself awaking to the implications of certain ideas I first encountered in graduate school. At the time, I never could have convinced any professor that I fully grasped them. Sometimes it takes an event later in life to trigger the learning—the "Oh, now I get it! So that's what he was talking about!" phenomenon. Was it poor teaching? Not in the least. It was highly effective and deeply imprinted. But the student couldn't have passed the test.

When is a lesson learned? A lesson may have been highly effective, but the effect may be dormant for years.

So far, I have been pointing only to fairly obvious problems with evaluations that the reader may have encountered often before. But there are other, more difficult, paradoxical issues. For example, take the paradoxical idea that *the opposite of a profound truth is also true.* Architect Mies van der Rohe's famous truth "Less is more" is surely profound. But less is also less. Or this one: "Beauty is in the eye of the beholder." Was there ever a more profound truth? But beauty is also in the object. If a profound truth (and presumably that is what we teachers want to convey) is also true in its opposite, then how do we evaluate a student who expresses the opposite, especially when the student may be expressing the more unconventional of the two. Suppose a student, responding to a test question, were to be the first to articulate the statement, "Beauty is in the eye of the beholder." That jarring truth would not be considered a correct answer. How do we evaluate a student when the answer is more profound than the question? Embarrassing as that may be, isn't it exactly what we would love to happen with our students?

Often the learning is not represented in the curriculum at all, but in the interstices between elements or ideas, or hidden somewhere in a seemingly idle remark. It may be true that most of our significant learning comes not directly from teachers, but from deep within ourselves as some situation we encounter enables us to formulate an idea that we didn't know resided in us. That is why I prefer to address an audience from notes rather than reading a prepared text— I may say something I didn't know that I knew.

FAILURE AS A NECESSARY STEP TO SUCCESS

With evaluation being such a fundamental part of the education system, failure is measured, graded, and penalized. If failure were seen rather as a necessary step toward success—which is the way it is viewed in the high-tech industries most dependent upon innovation—it would not lead to the devastating punishment of repeating a grade or a class or a test, enduring corporal punishment or other penalties at home, or dropping out. Failure in those innovative industries is not judged but analyzed, becoming the basis for learning and further experimentation. But failure in school is humiliating at best and severely damaging at worst. While not all failure is well-intended or benign, it all has meaning and relevance that deserves understanding.

In recent decades, the evaluative emphasis has been placed on what psychologists call positive reinforcement—rewarding the desired behavior. These extrinsic rewards—"A" grades, gold stars, honors and awards, even praise—have, however, all been shown to be counterproductive to learning. The student works for the reward rather than progress in learning, and quits when the reward is achieved. Students' eyes are on the reward rather than the work. These extrinsic rewards tend not to have the power of the intrinsic reward that comes from accomplishment in the work itself.

To show how we must regard failure in school, and in the educational system as a whole, perhaps we can use an analogy with the criminal justice system. When we decriminalize a crime—say, drug use or prostitution—we immediately take away the worst punishment. It is no longer cause for arrest and prison. Going a step further, however, if we legitimize that previously criminal behavior, we are actually accommodating it, finding ways to treat it, but still not condoning it. With failure, we have to go even further. We have to welcome it, embrace it, use it, study and analyze it, build on it . . . thus removing the stigma entirely.

WHAT TEACHERS REALLY TEACH

Students learn in many ways. As we have mentioned, they learn from themselves. They also learn from each other. Students at all levels, from kindergarten through graduate school, learn more from each other than from their teachers.

Still, the teacher plays a crucially important role. But it isn't the role that most people, including the teachers themselves, think they play. It's a much richer, more profound role, because the scripted performance is not what their students learn. Teaching is more like parenthood. What parents deliberately *do* as a parenting skill matters little in what their children become. But what their parents *are* matters a great deal. That is what children learn and become. Children always learn who their parents really are, even if the parents sometimes wish that weren't true. The same is true for teachers. The students learn who their teachers are, and that can be highly influential in many directions.

That's why it is unfortunate that teachers are saddled with so many curricular goals and disciplinary burdens instead of being able to express themselves and their own strong interests. It is especially discouraging to note that teachers are increasingly frustrated by having to place discipline ahead of teaching and engage in practices they know are unsupported by research, such as grading, homework, and curricular limitations that are politically mandated. Teachers do not want to constantly be in an evaluative relationship to their students.

Yet, evaluation seems so rational. After all, how can students know how they are doing without evaluation? And how would we make decisions about extending contracts or giving tenure without evaluation? How else can we hold people in the system accountable? The rational defense of evaluation seems overwhelming. But human affairs do not operate rationally; they operate paradoxically. In human experience, paradox is the rule, not the exception. So rational evaluation is always likely to be off the mark.

Every teacher knows that Einstein and Edison did not do

What all of us need—students, teachers, and administrators—is not evaluation but engagement.

well in school, and that Bill Gates and Steve Jobs dropped out of college, but teachers can seldom apply that understanding to their present students. Indeed, the system hardly lets them.

What all of us need—students, teachers, and administrators—is not evaluation but *engagement*. We need to be encouraged to take risks, and when the effort doesn't work or a mistake is made, we don't need judgment, we need understanding. We need to analyze the failure in the company of our teacher or boss and see what we can learn from it. That is what the better teachers, and better bosses, have always done. Evaluation is cheap and easy and superficial. Engagement is more demanding, but far more rewarding.

Essentially we need to treat success and failure similarly, neither rewarding one nor punishing the other. Better that we treat them non-judgmentally, with genuine engagement.

THE PROBLEM OF STANDARDS

Schooling should neither be compulsory nor standardized. Our moving social consciousness will eventually get around to recognizing children in the way we have recently recognized the need for a revolutionized perspective toward African Americans, women, and gays and lesbians. At that time, children will be given the full protection of the Constitution and compulsory education will be ended as a matter of children's rights. (Doesn't "compulsory education" sound like an oxymoron?) At this point, however, there is little that educators can do about that problem, so they continually suffer with classroom control of incarcerated students being more important than learning. Standardization, however, is something they can resist, but not because they tend to believe in it themselves. After all, shouldn't we make sure that all students acquire the skills that will be necessary as they move along? And don't standards set appropriate goals for learning?

Not really. Standards tend to be minimal, not high, and certainly not challenging to the brightest and most motivated. To base graduation on the completion of minimal standards is to them demeaning. It is no accident that child prodigies are often home schooled. The problem is similar to professional licensing. The profession thinks licensing increases the respect that society will have for it, and that the physicians or architects or other professionals will respect themselves and each other more. But it actually works the other way around. Licensing has reduced public regard; no professionals worth their salt point to their license as proof of competence. They point to their work, or to the esteem of their colleagues. They would never suggest to a friend who has asked for a referral that he or she should just seek out a licensed professional.

WHAT STUDENTS LEARN

Students do not learn what is in the curriculum. As the social critic Ivan Illich pointed out, they learn what is in the "hidden curriculum," the metamessage sent by the ritual and form of education. They learn to sit still, raise their hands, obey adult authority, stand in line, take turns, and so forth. They learn what kind of people the teachers really are, not just what they know about the curriculum. That is the metamessage that the teacher sends, and it is what the students learn, for better or worse.

Naturally we want teachers who know the subject being taught, but perhaps even more we need teachers who know something of interest to share with the students, whether it is in the standard curriculum or not—astronomy, bird watching, dancing, environmental management, whatever. We need teachers who can make learning exciting because they are excited. In that process, we learn that there are many avenues to the basics.

Having said that, I do want to recognize the place of expertise, of structure, of subject matter that has been deemed important for centuries, and of the dedicated work of educators who have organized curricular material in ways that make it accessible. But to have those resources, we do not need evaluation as it is now practiced. If we deem it important that students receive feedback on their progress (which they seldom need because they already know), it is possible to make that feedback self-administered or automated, removing both the teacher from the evaluative relationship and the oppressive grading system itself.

The lucky students find themselves with teachers who have inquiring minds, who are themselves learners, and who are willing to take their students on that learning journey.

The great lesson in management is to recognize the natural coexistence of opposites, of freedom and limits, and the inevitable paradoxes in life. The best leaders are able to go in seemingly opposite directions at once. Yes, we need teachers who bring something special of themselves to the learning situation. Also, we need organization, the discipline of a curriculum, and attention to subject matter that has stood the tests of time. These concerns are not mutually exclusive. There is even a term for them: simultaneous management.

The lucky students find themselves with teachers who have inquiring minds, who are themselves learners, and who are willing to take their students on that learning journey. I would much prefer that my children be placed in the company of teachers who will engage them and who have inquiring minds, even if the teachers' interests often depart from the standard curriculum. Unfortunately, the current design of the educational system does not attract such inquiring minds. The education departments on most university campuses rank at the bottom, settling for the least qualified students, the fewest inquiring minds.

EDUCATORS AS PROFESSIONALS

All this makes it difficult for teachers and administrators to stand up as professionals and insist on their judgment prevailing. Teaching is one of the few professions dominated by its clientele. Its professional societies, like most professional associations, are mainly protective of the incomes of their members. The mark of professionals is the ability to say "No" to what they have reason to believe is a mistaken action. Instead, teachers and administrators continue to offer programs that meet the demands of parents or school boards, such as assigning grades and homework, when they know it is not only irrelevant to the learning process, but creates an ordeal for both parent

Ordeal is not a strong enough word to convey the crippling pain and humiliation experienced by students who are stigmatized by failure.

and teacher, to say nothing of what the student goes through. And ordeal is not a strong enough word to convey the crippling pain and humiliation experienced by students who are stigmatized by failure or segregated into special education, when actually every student should have special education.

I'm well aware of the fact that evaluation is embedded in the larger system that surrounds our schooling. It is tied to college entry, scholarships and financial aid, job interviews and vocational placement, school advancement, teacher and administrator assessment, and accreditation and government financing. The list goes on. Even if educators were doubtful of its value, one could easily understand why they would throw up their hands at the complications of eliminating, or even reducing, evaluation in schools.

Incorporating failure as a plus, not a minus, is therefore a rather intimidating prospect, even if educators were convinced that evaluation is not necessary. Obviously that conviction, that motivation, if it exists, has not been sufficient, because evaluation and grading have come under severe criticism for generations, without ensuing change. But I cannot help but think that if we genuinely believed that evaluation truly is poisonous—that it is ruining lives—we would take action. Well, it is poisonous. It does ruin lives.

None of us wants a system that homogenizes its people, losing some of its best teachers and students, casting off its deviant or failing members, but that is what we have. It is the direct consequence of standards, evaluation, and risk aversion, and it is dangerous for our civilization for us to continue this way. We need organizations that help create people who can take our society to places we have never dreamed of. It has been an entire century since we have produced people who have contributed truly civilization-changing ideas—people like Freud, Einstein, Darwin, Edison, and Gandhi. We need for some of our students to leap ahead of all of us. We need to develop a system that not only permits that, but *encourages* it—not with honors and awards, but with the freedom and encouragement that comes from non-judgmental interest.

TAKING ACTION

What has to happen for us to make progress in reinventing the educational system to make more innovation possible? Probably the first step is to engage in an exercise of imagination. What would it be like to adopt a different posture toward failure, toward the entire system of evaluation? What can we change, and what must we keep? No doubt we can be helped by considering the research on what really matters in education, how we might better integrate the school with the family and community, call upon unused community resources, work more with laypeople and paraprofessionals, use the global reach of the Internet, and rely more on student-centered teaching and upon students learning from each other.

What would it be like to adopt a different posture toward failure, toward the entire system of evaluation?

Second, we must recognize a basic truth: Under the current design, we will never have enough teachers to do the job. Elevating teachers to positions of highly compensated leadership is long overdue. They should become managers, directing the work of paraprofessionals, community members, and other lay and volunteer resources, sometimes by managing new communication technologies, so that the term "individualized instruction" takes on real meaning. They must become metaprofessionals—working for the same goals but at a higher level. As managers, they will have additional cause to embrace the value of failure.

Third, we need our teachers and administrators to be able to stand up for what they know to be valuable, and to reject what they know to be counterproductive. They must be empowered to say "No." It is clearly too much to ask them to risk this individually, but with the backing of their professional associations, they would be in a much stronger position. Perhaps these associations can be moved beyond the protectionist stands they now feature to give greater support to the professional judgment of their members.

Fourth, perhaps we can become less intimidated by the way evaluation is embedded into the systems that articulate with schools. Some radical changes can be made by individual schools or districts, but other improvements will require the development of a critical mass of cooperating school systems. Without such a critical mass of educational institutions deciding together to alter the grading procedures now in place, the college-bound graduates of a single school that undertook such a program would be unfairly penalized. But if enough systems decided to discontinue grading and to not supply grade-point averages to college admissions offices, do we imagine that the colleges will close? Hardly. They might find better ways to assemble their student bodies. Remember, they too are burdened by the same dysfunctional evaluation system. Here again, actions by the broadly based professional societies could be helpful. Indeed, even the colleges themselves could be helpful in a collaborative redesign of the admissions system.

Other problems may be easier to solve. If the organizations that bestow honors and awards are unable to do so, all the better. Such extrinsic rewards are counterproductive to education. Financial aid can be granted without resorting to grades as the only measure of commitment to schooling. Scholarships can and should be awarded on criteria other than grades. Accreditation and accountability are highly questionable activities, and in any case need not be dependent upon grading. Federal and state governments, school boards, and even parents may eventually support better educational plans that are solidly based on research. Considerable evidence to the contrary should not force us to abandon that hope.

We are not paralyzed in any case. The acceptance of failure can play a major role in improving education, even without any change in current systems of grading students. Teachers, administrators, and school board members can encourage more risk taking within the organization, and offer support and genuine engagement when failure occurs. That attitude can become contagious. It is happening in business organizations all over the world.

Democracy will always be messy, and partisan politics will always play a role, even though evaluation, per se, is not necessarily a partisan issue. Will we encounter strong resistance, argument, outrage? Of course. Will we become frustrated and discouraged? Surely. Can the educational system continue as it is? Probably—it has for centuries. School is where the public wants its children to be, even if they learn little more than is in the hidden curriculum. Can we do better? Unquestionably. Much better. But only by failing more.

If all this seems too great a task, remember one final paradox: *Big changes are easier to make than small ones.*

INDEX

CORWIN
PRESS

The Corwin Press logo—a raven striding across an open book—represents the union of courage and learning. Corwin Press is committed to improving education for all learners by publishing books and other professional development resources for those serving the field of PreK–12 education. By providing practical, hands-on materials, Corwin Press continues to carry out the promise of its motto: **"Helping Educators Do Their Work Better."**

The HOPE Foundation logo stands for Harnessing Optimism and Potential Through Education. The HOPE Foundation helps to develop and support educational leaders over time at district- and state-wide levels to create school cultures that sustain all students' achievement, especially low-performing students.

The American Association of School Administrators, founded in 1865, is the professional organization for more than 13,000 educational leaders across America and in many other countries. AASA's mission is to support and develop effective school system leaders who are dedicated to the highest quality public education for all children.

NATIONAL ASSOCIATION OF ELEMENTARY SCHOOL PRINCIPALS
Serving All Elementary and Middle Level Principals

The 29,500 members of the National Association of Elementary School Principals provide administrative and instructional leadership for public and private elementary and middle schools throughout the United States, Canada, and overseas. Founded in 1921, NAESP is today a vigorously independent professional association with its own headquarters building in Alexandria, Virginia, just across the Potomac River from the nation's capital. From this special vantage point, NAESP conveys the unique perspective of the elementary and middle school principal to the highest policy councils of our national government. Through national and regional meetings, award-winning publications, and joint efforts with its 50 state affiliates, NAESP is a strong advocate both for its members and for the 33 million American children enrolled in preschool, kindergarten, and grades 1 through 8.